The Children Act 1989 & Child Protection

Fergus Smith

B.Sc.(Hons), M.A., C.Q.S.W., D.M.S., Dip.M

CAe

Children Act Enterprises Ltd
Pantiles
Langham Road
Robertsbridge
East Sussex TN32 5EP
tel: 01580 880243

www.caeuk.org

British Library Cataloguing in Publication Data
A catalogue record for this book is available from the British
Library

ISBN 978 1 899986 48 4

Designed and typeset by Helen Joubert Design
Printed in the UK by The Lavenham Press

CAE is an independent organisation which publishes guides
to family and criminal law and provides consultancy,
research, training and independent investigation services to
the public, private and voluntary sectors.

Contents

Regulations are 'subordinate' legislation which must be obeyed.

'Statutory Guidance' is Government advice which does not have the force of law, but should be complied with unless local circumstances indicate exceptional reasons justifying a variation.

'Public law' refers to services the State provides for families and the procedures followed by the State to protect children when families fail to do so. 'Private law' is concerned with the allocation of responsibility/resolution of disputes between parents and/or other individuals.

When case law is referred to:
All ER = All England Law Reports
EHRR = European Human Rights Reports
EWCA Civ = Court of Appeal civil Division
Fam. = Official law reports: Family Division of High Court
Fam. Law = Family Law
FCR = Family Court Reports
FLR = Family Law Reports

Other abbreviations used are:
ECHR = European Convention for the Protection of Human Rights and Fundamental Freedoms
ACA 2002 = Adoption and Children Act 2002
ASCLA 2009 = Apprenticeship, Skills & Learning Act 2009
CA 1989 = Children Act 1989

CA 2004 = Children Act 2004
CAA 2006 = Children and Adoption Act 2006
CCA 2006 = Childcare Act 2006
CDA 2008 = Crime & Disorder Act 2008
CFA 2014 = Children and Families Act 2014
CJCA 2000 = Criminal Justice & courts act 2000
CPA 2004 = Civil Partnership Act 2004
C&YPA 2008 = Children & Young Persons Act 2008
EA 2002 = Education Act 2002
FLA 1996 = Family Law Act 1996
FLRA 1969 = Family Law Reform Act 1969
FLRA 1987 = Family Law Reform Act 1987
OMA 2007 = Offender Management Act 2007
PHA 1997 = Protection from Harassment Act 1997
HRA 1998 = Human Rights Act 1998
POCA 1999 = Protection of Children Act 1999
SOA 2003 = Sexual Offences Act 2003
SVGA 2006 = Safeguarding Vulnerable Groups Act 2006

The text reflects statute (insofar as Commencement
Orders have been issued) and the most significant case
law as at 01.09.14.

The guide should be used only to supplement
regulations, guidance and local policies and procedures.

Introduction

■ This guide is designed for use by those in England (and Wales) who plan, develop or deliver social care or safeguarding services to children and their families e.g:

- Chief Executives, Directors of Children's Services (DCS), chairpersons of Local Safeguarding Children Board (LSCBs)
- Managers in Children's Social Care, Health Commissioners/Providers, Police and Probation
- Doctors, nurses, health visitors, social workers and teachers

■ Part A provides access to, and reinforces understanding of the Children Act 1989, including major amendments introduced by the Children and Families Act 2014 and the most significant case law.

■ Part B includes the previously separate 'Personal Guide to Child Protection' and reflects the latest 2013 edition of *Working Together to Safeguard Children* as well as other statutory guidance subsequently issued

■ The guide also recognises the implications of the Children (Leaving Care) Act 2000, Care Standards Act 2000, Adoption and Children Act 2002, Carers and Disabled Children Act 2000, Civil Partnership Act 2004, Children and Adoption Act 2006, Children and Young Persons Act 2008 and Care Planning, Placement and Review (England) 2010 (as amended).

- Appendix 1 provides a summary of relevant Articles and Protocols of the European Convention on Human Rights and appendix 2 a summary of the Human Rights Act 1998 which brought the provisions of the Convention into UK law on 02.10.00.

A

CHILDREN ACT 1989: GENERAL PROVISIONS

Key Points of Children Act 1989 as amended

■ The child's welfare is paramount and safeguarding and promoting it is the priority.

NB. It has been suggested that this may conflict with parents' rights under Article 8(1) of the Convention which provides for the right to respect for family life [Hendriks v Netherlands [1982] 5 EHRR 223].

Others conclude that paramountcy is consistent with Convention case-law, within the 'margin of appreciation' permitted national authorities under Article 8(2) and therefore compatible with the right to respect for family life [Lord Hobhouse in Dawson v Wearmouth [1999] in FLR 167 who stated that 'there is nothing in the Convention which requires the courts of this country to act otherwise than in accordance with the interests of the child'].

LJ Butler-Sloss in the Court of Appeal stated that where there was a conflict of interest between the rights and interests of a child and those of a parent, the interests of the child had to prevail under Article 8(2) of the European Convention [Re L, V, M and H [2000] FLR 334]

■ Local authorities have a duty to ensure that support services for 'children in need' are provided and should minimise unnecessary intrusion into family life.

- Delay in resolution of court proceedings and provision of service must be avoided.

  NB. This principle received further reinforcement by the incorporation of Article 6 of the Convention which provides for the right to a fair trial within a reasonable time [see below for further discussion].

- Service providers must listen to and work in partnership with children and parents, any who have parental responsibility and relevant others.

- Needs arising from race, culture, religion and language must be taken into account by service providers and courts.

- A court (in considering contested s.8 Orders, or their contested variation or discharge, or award and removal of parental responsibility) will *presume* that unless the contrary is shown, involvement of a parent in the life of the child concerned will further her/his welfare.

Definitions

Care Plan [s.31A CA 1989 as inserted by s.121 ACA 2002]

■ When an application is made which might result in a Care Order, the appropriate local authority (the one proposed to be designated in the Order) must, within a time-scale directed by the court prepare a 'care plan' (referred to in the ACA 2002 as a 's.31A plan') for the future care of the child.

■ While the application is pending, the local authority must keep the plan under review and revise or replace it if this is required.

NB. A care plan must give any prescribed information and do so in the prescribed manner.

Child [s.105 (1) CA 1989]

■ For the purposes of child protection, a 'child' is a person of less than 18 years of age without regard to whether s/he is living independently, is in further education, in hospital or custody in the secure estate for children/young people or is a member of the Armed Forces.

'Child in Need' [s.17 (10); (11) CA 1989]

■ A child is 'in need' if:

   • S/he is unlikely to achieve or maintain, or have the opportunity to so do, a reasonable standard of health or development without provision of services by a local authority, or if

- Her/his health or development is likely to be significantly impaired, or further impaired, without such services, or
- S/he is disabled

NB. Health = physical or mental; Development = physical, intellectual, emotional, social or behavioural; Disabled = blind, deaf, dumb or suffering from mental disorder of any kind or substantially and permanently handicapped by illness, injury or congenital deformity, or other such disability as may be prescribed.

- Each local authority has a general duty to safeguard and promote welfare of children in need in its area, and so far as is consistent with that duty, promote their upbringing by their families by providing a range and level of services appropriate to their needs [s.17 (1) CA 1989].

  NB. A child who is at risk of 'significant harm' (see below) may be assumed to be a child in need and therefore eligible for family support services.

- Such children include those in Young Offender Institutions (YOIs) and in young persons' wings of prisons.

Child Protection

- Child protection is a part of 'safeguarding and promoting welfare'. It refers to the activity that is undertaken to protect children who are suffering, or are likely to suffer, significant harm. Effective child protection is essential as part of wider work to safeguard and promote the welfare of children. All agencies and individuals should aim proactively to safeguard and promote the welfare of children so that the need for action to protect children from harm is reduced.

Child Protection Plan

- The 'core group' (see below) is responsible for developing the 'outline child protection plan' agreed at an initial child protection conference into a 'child protection plan' which sets out what work needs to be done, why, when and by whom.

- The overall aim of the plan is to:
  - Ensure the child is safe and prevent her/him from suffering further harm by supporting the strengths, addressing the vulnerabilities and risk factors and helping meet the child's unmet needs
  - Promote the child's health and development i.e. welfare and
  - Provided it is in her/his best interests, support the family and wider family members to safeguard and promote the welfare of their child

- The full child protection plan should:
  - Describe the identified developmental needs of the child and what therapeutic services are required

- Include specific, achievable, child-focused outcomes intended to safeguard and promote her/his welfare
- Include realistic strategies and specific actions to achieve planned outcomes
- Set out when and in what situations the child will be seen by the lead social worker, both alone and with other family members or caregivers present
- Clearly identify roles and responsibilities of professionals and family members, including those with routine contact with the child e.g. health visitors, GPs and teachers and the nature and frequency of contact by those professionals with child and family members
- Include a contingency plan to be followed if circumstances change significantly and require prompt action, including initiating family court proceedings to safeguard and promote the child's welfare
- Lay down points at which progress will be reviewed and the means by which progress will be judged

■ The plan should also:

- Take into account the wishes and feelings of the child and of the parent/s insofar as they are consistent with the child's welfare
- Be explained to the family via the lead social worker so that they understand the required

> outcomes and accept and are willing to work to the plan
> * Be provided in the family's preferred language

■ If families' preferences are not accepted, reasons should be provided and they should be told of their right to complain or make representations and how to do so.

Children's Services Authority (CSA)

■ A CSA in England is defined by s.65 CA 2004 as a:

* County council
* Metropolitan district council
* Non metropolitan district council for an area where there is no county council i.e. a unitary
* A London borough council
* The Common Council of the City of London and
* The Isles of Scilly

Civil Partnership

■ The Civil Partnership Act 2004 (CPA 2004) introduced into English law the concept of the 'civil partnership'.

■ S.1 CPA 2004 thus provides that 'a civil partnership' is a relationship between 2 same-sex 'civil partners' formed when they register as civil partners of each other in England and Wales under Part 2 of the Act.

■ This allowed, for the first time in UK law official legal recognition of the relationship of same sex couples to be accorded, provided the couple has registered the relationship under the provisions of CPA 2004.

Clinical Commissioning Groups (CCGs)

■ With effect from April 2013 CCGs became the major commissioners of local health services and are responsible for safeguarding quality assurance through contractual arrangements with all provider organisations.

Common Assessment Framework (CAF)

■ The CAF is a tool to enable early and effective assessment of children and young people who need additional services or support from more than one agency.

■ CAF is a holistic consent-based assessment framework which records, in a single place and in a structured and consistent way, every aspect of a child's life, family and environment.

NB. Children's Trust Boards should have clear arrangements in place for local implementation of CAF. A CAF is not a referral form though it may be used to support a referral or a specialist assessment.

Core Group

■ The core group is responsible for developing an outline protection plan into a full child protection plan that can be used as a working tool.

- Membership should include the lead social worker who chairs the core group, the child if appropriate, family members and professionals/foster carers who will have direct contact with the family.

- Although the lead social worker has lead responsibility, for the formulation and implementation of the child protection plan, all members are collectively responsible for carrying out these tasks, refining the plan as needed and monitoring progress against planned outcomes.

- Agencies should ensure that members of the core group undertake their roles and responsibilities effectively in accordance with the agreed child protection plan.

- The first core group meeting (to be convened within 10 working days of the initial conference) is to flesh out the protection plan and decide what steps need to be taken by whom to complete the core assessment on time. Thereafter, core groups should meet sufficiently regularly to facilitate working together, monitor actions and outcomes against the protection plan and make any necessary alterations as circumstances change.

  NB. The lead social worker should record decisions taken and actions agreed as well as written views of those unable to attend. The child protection plan should be updated as necessary.

'Designated' Professionals

■ All clinical commissioning groups (CCGs) should employ or have a contractual agreement to secure the expertise of a 'designated' doctor and nurse for safeguarding children and for looked after children (as well as designated paediatrician for unexpected deaths in childhood).

Emotional Abuse

■ Emotional abuse is the persistent emotional ill treatment of a child such as to cause severe and persistent effects on the child's emotional development. It may:

- Involve conveying to children that they are worthless or unloved, inadequate, or valued only insofar as they meet the needs of another person
- Include not giving the child opportunities to express views, deliberately silencing her/him or 'making fun' of what s/he says or how s/he communicates
- Feature age or developmentally inappropriate expectations being imposed on a child, including interactions that are beyond the child's capability as well as overprotection and limitation of exploration and learning, or preventing her/him participating in normal social interaction
- Involve seeing or hearing the ill-treatment of another person, involve serious bullying (including cyber-bullying) causing children to feel

frightened or in danger or the exploitation or corruption of children

■ Some level of emotional abuse is involved in all types of ill treatment of children, though emotional abuse may occur alone.

Family [s.17]

■ For purposes of providing support services, the term family includes any person with parental responsibility and anyone with whom the child has been living.

Joint Strategic Needs Assessment (JSNA)

■ The Local Government and Public Involvement in Health Act 2007 requires Clinical Commissioning Groups and local authorities to produce a Joint Strategic Needs Assessment (JSNA) of the health and wellbeing of their local community.

■ The director of Public Health should ensure that the needs of vulnerable children are a key part of the JSNA that is developed by the Health & Wellbeing Board.

Lead Member

■ The lead Member for Children's Services has delegated responsibility from the Council for children, young people and their families and is politically accountable for ensuring that the local authority fulfils its legal responsibilities for safeguarding and promoting the welfare of children and young people.

■ The lead Member should provide the political leadership needed for the effective co-ordination of work with other relevant agencies that have safeguarding responsibilities e.g. Police, and Health Services.

■ The lead Member should also take steps to assure her/himself that effective quality assurance systems for safeguarding are in place and functioning effectively.

Lead Social Worker

■ The lead social worker (a registered social worker from Children's Social Care or NSPCC) is responsible for making sure that the outline child protection plan is developed into a more detailed inter-agency plan and has the lead role in inter-agency work with the family.

■ S/he should complete the core assessment of child/ family securing contributions from core group members and other as necessary and review progress against the agreed objectives.

■ The lead social worker is also responsible for acting as the lead professional for inter-agency work with child and family.

NB. This role should be fully explained at the initial child protection conference and at the core group.

Local Authority [s.105 CA 1989]

■ The term 'local authority' in the Children Act 1989 means a county council, metropolitan district, London borough or a unitary authority, not just Children's Social Care.

Looked After Child [s.22 CA 1989]

■ Children 'looked after' by a local authority may be 'accommodated', 'in care' or 'remanded/detained'.

■ Accommodation is a voluntary arrangement in which the local authority does not gain parental responsibility and no notice is required for removal of the child.

■ 'In care' means that a court has made a child subject of a Care Order which gives the local authority parental responsibility and (some) authority to limit parents' exercise of their continuing parental responsibility.

■ A local authority is authorised to detain those in the third category who may acquire such status as a result of:

- Remand by a court following criminal charges
- Detention following arrest by police
- An Emergency Protection Order (which also awards temporary parental responsibility to the local authority) or Child Assessment Order
- A 'criminal' Supervision Order with a residence requirement

NB. S.22 (1) (b) as amended by s.2 Children (Leaving Care) Act 2000 enables the local authority to provide accommodation for a child who has left its care without her/him being considered 'looked after'.

Named Professional

■ All providers of NHS funded health services, including NHS and NHS Foundation Trusts, public, voluntary sector, independent sector and social enterprises should identify a 'named' doctor and a named nurse (plus a named midwife if the organisation provided maternity services) for safeguarding.

■ In the case of NHS '111' Service, Ambulance Trusts and independent providers, this should be a named professional.

■ GP practices should have a lead and a deputy lead for safeguarding, who should work closely with named GPs.

■ Named professionals have a key role in promoting good professional practice within the organisation, providing advice and expertise for colleagues and ensuring safeguarding training is in place.

■ The named professional should work closely with the safeguarding lead, designated professionals and LSCB.

NB. Model job descriptions for designated and named professional roles may be found in the inter-collegiate document 'Safeguarding Children and Young People: roles and competencies for health care staff' September 2010 at www.rcph.ac.uk/

Neglect

■ Neglect is the persistent failure to meet a child's basic physical and/or psychological needs, likely to result in the serious impairment of health and development.

■ Neglect may occur during pregnancy as a result of maternal substance abuse.

■ Neglect may involve a parent or carer failing to:

- Provide adequate food and clothing
- Provide shelter e.g. exclusion from home or abandonment
- Protect a child from physical and emotional harm or danger or
- Ensure adequate supervision including use of inadequate care takers or

- Ensure access to appropriate medical care/ treatment, and may include neglect/ unresponsiveness to basic emotional needs)

■ Evidence of neglect is built up over time and can cover a range of parenting tasks.

No Delay Principle [s.1 (2) CA 1989]

■ In all court proceedings, delay is presumed to be prejudicial, though this presumption can be rebutted if the delay is a constructive one [Re B (A Minor) (Contact) (Interim Order) 1994 2 FLR].

NB. Article 6 of the Convention (Right to Fair Trial)

Parent Carer [s.17ZD(2) inserted by s.97 CFA 2014]

■ A 'parent carer' means a person aged 18 or over who provides or intends to provide care for a disabled child for whom the person has parental responsibility.

Outline Child Protection Plan

■ Following a decision made at an initial or review conference that a child does need or continues to need a protection plan, an 'outline child protection plan' should:

- Identify risk and protective factors based upon current findings from the assessment and information held from any previous involvement with child and family

- Establish short and long-term aims and objectives that are clearly linked to reducing the likelihood of harm to the child and promoting her/his welfare, including contact with family members
- Be clear about who will have responsibility for what actions – including actions by family members – within what timescales
- Outline ways of monitoring and evaluating progress against planned outcomes in the plan
- Be clear about which professional is responsible for checking that the required changes have taken place and what action will be taken, by whom when they have not

Paramountcy of Child's Welfare [s.1 (1) CA 1989]

■ When a court determines any question with respect to a child's upbringing or administration of property or income, her/his welfare must be the paramount consideration.

■ In cases where the s.1 (1) criteria apply and the interests of two or more children conflict, it is for the court to reach a decision based on a balancing exercise [see dicta of Balcombe LJ in Birmingham City Council v H (NO.2) 1 FLR 883 1993].

■ The House of Lords has confirmed that where both parent and child are 'children' within the meaning of the Act, the child's needs are paramount [Birmingham City Council v H (NO.2) [1993]1 FLR 883 HL].

- It has been accepted by the Court of Appeal that a Parental Responsibility Order relates to the upbringing of a child so is governed by the paramountcy principle [Re G (A Minor) (Parental Responsibility Order) [1994] 1 FLR 504] and the A (Conjoined Twins) [2001] FLR].

- Lord Hobhouse in Dawson v Wearmouth and the Court of Appeal in Re L, V, M and H (see p. 4) indicate the paramountcy principle can be read into Article 8(2) which provides the qualifications for interference with the rights laid down in Article 8(1).

Parental Responsibility [s.3 CA 1989]

- 'Parental responsibility' means all the rights, duties, powers, responsibilities and authority which by law a parent has in relation to a child and her/his property.

Physical Abuse

- Physical abuse may involve hitting, shaking, throwing, poisoning, burning or scalding, drowning, suffocating or otherwise causing physical harm to a child.

- Physical harm may also be caused when a parent or carer feigns symptoms of, or deliberately causes, ill-health to a child (variously described as 'fabricated or induced illness').

Positive Advantage [s.1 (5)]

- A court cannot make any order unless it considers to do so would be better than making no order.

'Preventable' Child Death

■ Those in which modifiable factors may have contributed. These factors are defined as those which, by means of nationally or locally achievable interventions, could be modified to reduce the risk of future child deaths.

■ In reviewing the death of each child, a Child Death Overview Panel (CDOP) should consider modifiable factors e.g. in the family and environment, parenting capacity or service provision, and consider what action could be taken locally and what action could be taken at a regional or national level.

Record that Child is Subject of a Child Protection Plan

■ Children's Social Care information technology (IT) systems should be capable of capturing in the child's case record whether s/he is subject of a child protection plan. Each local authority system which is supporting the Integrated Children's System (ICS) should be capable of producing a list of all those resident in the area (including any placed there by another local authority) considered to be at continuing risk of significant harm, and for whom there is a child protection plan.

■ The main purpose of having the above capacity is to enable agencies and professionals to be aware of those children assessed to be at continuing risk of significant harm and who are subject of a child protection plan.

■ Police and health professionals must be able to access the above information in and out of office hours.

Safeguarding

■ Safeguarding is defined in statutory guidance as:

- Protecting children from maltreatment
- Preventing impairment of their health or development
- Ensuring children are growing up in circumstances consistent with provision of safe and effective care and
- Taking action to enable children in need to have optimum life chances

Sexual Abuse

■ Sexual abuse involves forcing or enticing a child/ young person to participate in sexual activities (including being prostituted) whether or not s/he is aware of what is happening.

■ Activities may involve physical contact, including penetrative (e.g. rape or oral sex) or non-penetrative acts such as masturbation, kissing, rubbing and touching outside of clothing.

■ Sexual abuse may involve non-contact activities e.g. involving a child in looking at or in production of pornography, watching sexual activities or encouraging her/him to behave in sexually inappropriate ways or grooming her/him in preparation for abuse (including via the internet).

Sex Offender Register

- The notification requirements of Part 2 of the Sexual Offences Act 2003 (the sex offenders register) are an automatic requirement on offenders who receive a conviction or caution for certain sexual offences.

- The notification requirements are intended to ensure that the police are informed of the whereabouts of offenders in the community.

- Offenders must notify police of certain personal details within 3 days of conviction or caution for relevant sexual offences (or if in prison on that date, within 3 days of release).

- Such an offender must then notify police within 3 days of any change to the notified details and whenever s/he spends 7 days or more at another address. All offenders must re-confirm their details at least once every 12 months and notify police 7 days in advance of any travel overseas lasting 3 days or more.

- The period of time that an offender must comply with these requirements depends on whether they received a conviction or a caution and, where appropriate, the sentence received.

■ Notification requirements do not bar offenders from certain types of employment or from being alone with children.

NB. Failure to comply with these requirements is a criminal offence and Police should be contacted if such an offence is committed.

Significant Harm [s.31 (9) CA 1989 as amended by s.120 ACA 2002]

■ 'Significant harm' is the threshold which justifies compulsory intervention in family life.

■ Harm means ill-treatment or impairment of health or development (including impairment suffered from seeing or hearing ill-treatment of another).

■ Development means physical, intellectual, emotional, social or behavioural development and health means physical or mental health. Ill-treatment includes sexual abuse and forms of ill-treatment which are not physical.

■ Where the question of whether harm suffered by a child is significant turns on the child's health and development, her/his health or development must be compared with that which could reasonably be expected of a similar child [s.31(10) CA 1989].

'Unexpected' Death of a Child

■ The death of an infant or child (less than 18 years old) which was not anticipated as a significant possibility for example, 24 hours before the death, or where there was a similarly unexpected collapse or incident leading to or precipitating the events which led to the death.

■ The designated paediatrician responsible for unexpected deaths in childhood should be consulted if professionals are uncertain about whether a death is unexpected. If in doubt, the processes for unexpected child deaths should be followed until the available evidence enables a different decision to be made.

Welfare [s.1 (2A;2B) introduced by s.11 (2) CFA 2014) & Checklist [s.1 (3) CA 1989]

■ A court (in considering contested s.8 Orders, or their contested variation or discharge, or award and removal of parental responsibility) will *presume* that unless the contrary is shown, involvement of a parent in the life of the child concerned will further her/his welfare [s.1 (2A) CA 1989].

NB. Involvement means involvement of some kind, direct or indirect but not any particular division of a child's time [s.1 (2B)].

■ For the above purpose a parent is to be treated as being capable of being involved in the child's life in a way that does not put the child at risk of suffering significant harm *unless* there is some evidence before the court to suggest such involvement would put the child at risk of suffering significant harm, whatever the form of involvement [s.1 (6) inserted by s.11 CFA 2014].

■ In considering an opposed s.8 Order or Care or Supervision Order (including Interim Care and Supervision and Education Supervision Orders), the court must have regard to checklist of:

- Child's wishes/feelings
- Physical, emotional, educational needs
- Likely effect of change of circumstances
- Age, sex, background, relevant characteristics (this should include race, culture, religion and language)
- Actual or potential harm
- Capability of parents/relevant others to meet child's needs
- Available range of powers [s.1(3) CA 1989]

■ Although the child's wishes and feelings appear first, they have no priority over the others [Re W (A Minor) (Medical Treatment): Court's Jurisdiction) [1993] 1 FLR 1].

NB. In s.4 applications for Parental Responsibility Orders the court does not have to apply the statutory criteria of s.1 (3) and (4) but both court and parties ought to bear these criteria in mind when they may be relevant e.g. strongly expressed wishes of an older child.

Young Carer [s.17ZA;ZB inserted by s.96 CFA 2014]

- A young carer means a person under 18 who provides or intends to provide care for another person but does not do so under or by virtue of, a contract or as voluntary work.

PART 1: PARENTAL RESPONSIBILITY ETC

Parental Responsibility

Allocation in Case of Married Parents

■ If a child's parents were married to each other at any time following her/his conception they each have parental responsibility [s.2 (1) & s.1 FLRA 1987].

■ The Children Act 1989 emphasises the enduring nature of married parents' responsibility towards their child/ren which can be lost only if the child is freed for adoption, adopted, attains the age of 18 or dies.

■ Each parent/other person with parental responsibility can act independently in the exercise of it e.g. giving consent to medical treatment.

NB. In Re J (Specific Issue Order: Child's Religious Upbringing and Circumcision) 2000 1 FLR, Thorpe LJ and Dame Butler Sloss P in the Court of Appeal agreed there was a small group of important or exceptional decisions which ought not to be carried out without consent of all those who have parental responsibility, or a court.

Case law suggests these are irreversible actions e.g. circumcision and sterilisation but also includes: immunisation against infectious diseases [Re C [2003] 2FLR 1095] changes of surname [Re S [2001] 2 FLR 1005] or school or type of education [Re P [2003] 1 FLR 286, in which the Court of Appeal emphasised courts must not abdicate from their duty to decide such matters when parents cannot agree.

Allocation in Case of Civil Partners

■ If a child's parent (parent A) who has parental responsibility for the child is a civil partner of a person who is *not* the child's parent i.e. is a step-parent:

- Parent A (or if the other parent also has parental responsibility, both parents) may by agreement with the step-parent provide for her/him to have parental responsibility for the child [s.4A(1)(a)] or
- The court may, on the application of the step-parent, order that s/he has parental responsibility for the child [s.4A(1)(b) introduced by s.112 ACA 2002 and amended by s.75 CPA 2004]

NB. The CPA 2004 amended the definitions in s.105 (1) Children Act 1989 so that a 'child of the family' means with respect to those who are civil partners, a child of both of them, and any other child (other than one placed with them as foster carers by a local authority or voluntary organisation) who has been treated by them as a child of their family.

Divorce/ Dissolution of Civil Partnership

■ If a married couple separate or divorce, both continue to have parental responsibility for their child/ren.

■ Similarly, a couple in a registered civil partnership who have parental responsibility and separate or dissolve the partnership also retain parental responsibility.

■ Such couples are expected to agree suitable arrangements and court orders to determine with whom the child/ren should live, have contact or other related matters will only be made when necessary.

Allocation: Unmarried Woman & Man

■ If a child's mother and father were not married to each other at any time following her/his conception:

- The mother has parental responsibility for the child [s.2(2)(a)] and
- The father will have parental responsibility if he has acquired it and has not ceased to have it [s.2(2)(b) as amended by s.111 ACA 2002]

Acquisition of Parental Responsibility by Unmarried Father [s.4 as amended by s.111 ACA 2002]

■ s.4 has been amended by s.111 (1)–(3) ACA 2002 to allow an unmarried father to obtain parental responsibility, if:

- He registers as the father in England and Wales under specified sections of the Births and Deaths Registration Act 1953 (or equivalents in Scotland and Northern Ireland) [s.4(1)(a) CA 1989]

NB. For all children born after 01.12.03 if the father jointly registered the birth with the mother, he will have acquired automatic parental responsibility; for children born before 01.12.03 even if the father registered the birth jointly with the mother he will have to take positive steps to acquire such responsibility either by seeking re-registration under the terms of the Births and Deaths Registration Act 1953 or under the provisions of s.4 CA 1989]

- He and the mother make a 'parental responsibility agreement' providing for him to have parental responsibility [s.4(1)(b) CA 1989] or
- The court, on his application, orders that he shall have parental responsibility [s.4(1) (c) CA 1989

NB. An unmarried father could also acquire parental responsibility if the child's mother had appointed him in her will as the child's guardian, and subsequently died [s.5 (6) CA 1989].

- A person who has acquired parental responsibility as above, ceases to have it only if [s.4(2A) as substituted by s.111(4) ACA 2002] the court so orders on the application of:

  - Any person who has parental responsibility for the child or
  - With the leave of the court, the child her/himself

- It is possible for an unmarried father who acquires parental responsibility by any of the following means to subsequently lose it:

- A Parental Responsibility Agreement or Parental Responsibility Order
- A Child Arrangements Order
- Appointment as a guardian either by a court or in the mother's will

NB. In Re D (A Child) [2014] EWCA Civ 315 the Court of Appeal has upheld the decision of Baker J. to terminate the parental responsibility of a father who had been imprisoned for sexual offences against children from a previous relationship.

- If acquired by means of an appointment as guardian, the court could in 'Family Proceedings' and on its own initiative terminate appointment as the child's guardian.

- A father who acquires parental responsibility by jointly registering his child's birth with the mother can lose it *only* in the event of adoption, child's death or if the court so orders.

- The court should expressly consider, in the case of an application by an unmarried father, the degree of commitment he has shown the child, degree of attachment which exists and reasons for the application [S. v. R. (Parental Responsibility) [1993] 1 FCR 331].

- Tests of commitment, attachment and motivation are not exhaustive. Worrying injuries for which responsibility was not accepted justified refusal of the Order [Re H (Parental Responsibility) [1998] 1 FLR 855].

■ Denial of full contact [Re L (Contact: Trans-sexual
Applicant) [1995] 2 FLR 438] or acrimony between
parties [Re P (A Minor) (Parental Responsibility
Order) [1994] 1 FLR 578] are not necessarily bars to
a Parental Responsibility Order.

■ An example of a refusal to grant a Parental
Responsibility Order because of violence and the
applicant's refusal to comply with a court order for
maintenance exists [Re T (A Minor) (Parental
Responsibility: Contact) [1993] 1 FLR 450 CA].

*NB. The Welfare Reform Act 2009 introduced an
expectation that a mother registering the birth of her
baby should provide details of the father unless
specified criteria e.g. risk to her or the baby are
satisfied. Consultation on proposed 'Registration of
Births (Parents Not Married and Not Acting Together)
Regulations 2010 closed in February 2010 and final
regulations still remain to be implemented.*

Acquisition of Parental Responsibility by Step-Parent [s.4A inserted by s.112 ACA 2002]

■ s.4A has been amended by s.112 ACA 2002 to
provide that when a child's parent (parent A) who
has parental responsibility for the child, is married
to a person who is *not* the child's parent i.e. a
step-parent:

• Parent A (or if the other parent also has parental
responsibility, both parents) may by agreement
with the step-parent provide for her/him to have

parental responsibility for the child [s.4A(1)(a)] or

- The court may, on the application of the step-parent, order that s/he has parental responsibility for the child [s.4A(1)(b)]

▨ An agreement under s.4A(1)(a) is a 'Parental Responsibility Agreement' and must satisfy s.4(2) i.e. it must be in the form prescribed by the Lord Chancellor [s.4A(2) inserted by s.112 ACA 2002].

▨ A Parental Responsibility Agreement/Order under s.4A (1) (a) or (1) (b) respectively may only be brought to an end by an order of the court made on the application of any person who has parental responsibility, or with leave of the court the child her/himself [s.4A (3) (a)–(b)] and the court is satisfied that s/he has sufficient understanding to make the proposed application [s.4A (4)].

Effect of an Unmarried or a Step-Father Acquiring Parental Responsibility

▨ The essence of parental responsibility is that it is a status not merely a set of rights, duties and powers [Re S (Parental Responsibility) [1995] 2 FLR 648].

▨ Nonetheless, the practical advantages of such a status would include a right/ability to:

- Receive educational reports and provide consent to school trips
- Consent to treatment for, and receive medical reports about the child

- Sign official papers e.g. passport application
- Prevent a mother removing child from the UK
- Object to a proposed change of name
- Object to child's accommodation by local authority and an ability to lawfully remove her/him
- Be regarded as a 'parent' for purposes of adoption proceedings

NB. So as to comply with Article 8(1) of the Convention, best practice is to treat the unmarried father who does not have parental responsibility as possessing full rights in, e.g. adoption proceedings [see the statement to this effect by Butler-Sloss P in Re B [2002] 1FLR 365, which was not undermined by the House of Lords decision in the same case, reported [2002] 1FLR 196.

Acquisition of Parental Responsibility by Other Individuals

◼ An individual can also acquire parental responsibility if s/he is appointed as a child's guardian by a court or in writing, e.g. a will, by a person who has parental responsibility.

NB. This status takes effect only when both parents of a child are dead (unless the deceased parent had a Child Arrangements Order defining that the child was to live with her/him or s/he was the only parent with parental responsibility) [s.5 (7)]).

■ If the court makes a Child Arrangements Order with respect to a child, the father, or a woman who is the child's parent by virtue of s.43 HFEA 2008 is named in the Order as the person with whom the child is to live, and the father or the woman would not otherwise have parental responsibility for the child:

- The court must also make an order under s.4 giving the father (or under s.4ZA the woman) that responsibility [s.12 (1) as substituted by Sch.2 para. 21(2) CFA 2014].

■ If the court makes a Child Arrangements Order with respect to a child, the father, or a woman who is her/his parent by virtue of s.43 HFEA 2008 is named in the Order as the person with whom the child is to spend time or otherwise have contact but is *not* named in the Order as a person with whom the child is to live, and the father or the woman would not otherwise have parental responsibility for the child:

- The court must decide whether it would be appropriate, in view of the provision made in the Order to make an order under s.4 giving the father (or under s.4ZA the woman) that responsibility [s.12 (1A) as substituted by Sch.2 para. 21(2) CFA 2014]

NB. A guardian has all the powers of a parent with parental responsibility. A non-parent parental responsibility has a more limited for, e.g. s/he cannot consent to or refuse an application to free a child for adoption or adoption itself, nor appoint a guardian.

A guardian appointed by a parent or guardian (not by a court) has a right to disclaim her/his appointment 'within a reasonable time of first knowing that the appointment has taken effect' [s.6 (5)].

■ A non parent aged 18 or over can also acquire parental responsibility if an application to court is successful and a 'Special Guardianship Order' is made in her/his favour.

Acquisition of Parental Responsibility by Local Authority

■ A local authority obtains parental responsibility if a court makes a child subject of a 'Care Order' [s.33 (3)].

■ A Care Order does not remove a parent's parental responsibility and allows the local authority to determine, when satisfied it is necessary to safeguard or promote child's welfare, the extent to which parent/guardian may continue to meet her/his parental responsibility.

NB. A local authority with a Care Order cannot consent to or refuse an application to free a child for adoption, to adoption, appointment of a guardian or agree the child be brought up in a different religion [s.33(6)].

■ A local authority gains temporary parental responsibility if it obtains an Emergency Protection

Order (EPO) [s.44 (4)] or an Interim Care Order [Re B [2002] EWCA Civ 25 in the Times 29 January 2002].

- Even with an EPO, the authority can only exercise its parental responsibility to the extent reasonably required to safeguard or promote the child's welfare [s.44 (5)].

PART II: PART II ORDERS

s.8 Orders (as amended by s.12 CFA 2014]

- ■ The following orders are available to all levels of courts in private applications and Care and Supervision proceedings, *provided* the court is also satisfied that making an order is better than making no order at all.

- ■ With respect to a child 'in care' a court is empowered to grant *only* a Child Arrangements Order (and only if the arrangements regulated by that order relate to the issue of with whom the child is to live and/or when s/he is to do so). Such an order discharges the Care Order.

- ■ Other than in the case of a Child Arrangements Order, no court may make a s.8 order to last beyond the child's 16th birthday *unless* it is satisfied that the circumstances of the case are exceptional [s.9(6) as amended by s.37 C&YPA 2008 and Sch.2 para.].

  NB. Contact or Residence Orders made before implementation of the new provisions on 22.04.14 are deemed to be respectively a Child Arrangement Order in respect of either a). with whom and when the child is to spend time with or otherwise have contact with a person (old Contact Order) or b). with whom and when a child is to live with a person (old Residence Order).

Child Arrangements Order [s.8 CA 1989 as introduced by s.12 & Sch. 2 CFA 2014]

- A Child Arrangements Order means an order regulating arrangements about:
  - With whom a child is to live, spend time or otherwise have contact
  - When a child is to live, spend time or otherwise have contact with any person
- A Child Arrangements Order (insofar as it provides for the child to spend time or otherwise have contact with one of the child's parents at times when s/he is living with the child's other parent) will cease to have effect if parents resume cohabitation for at least 6 months [s.11(5) as substituted by Sch.2 para.6 CFA 2014].

Prohibited Steps Order [s.8(1) CA 1989 as amended]

■ A Prohibited Steps Order prevents someone from doing something which might ordinarily be done in fulfilling parental responsibility.

NB. Such an order must relate to an aspect of parental responsibility so (with some reservations) the House of Lords has determined that it could not include a ban on publicity [Re W (Wardship: Discharge: Publicity) [1995] 2 FLR 466].

The courts will have to bear in mind the provisions of Article 9 of the Convention (Right to Freedom of Thought, Conscience and Religion) when considering applications for Prohibited Steps or Specific Issue Orders [see decision in Re J (Circumcision) [2000] 1 FLR 571[CA].

Specific Issue Order [s.8(1) CA 1989 as amended]

- A Specific Issue Order resolves a particular problem e.g. education/medical treatment, or change of name.

- In Re A [2000] 1 FLR 121, the court granted a Specific Issue Order providing that children of a French father and English mother should attend a Lycee in London whilst living with their mother in order to reflect their part French parentage.

- Leave of a court to change a child's surname is required if a Child Arrangements Order is in force or there is disagreement between 2 or more people who have parental responsibility [s.13(1) as amended by Sch.1 para. 22 CFA 2014].

- Otherwise issues as to names should be dealt with as a Specific Issue Order sought by either parent as required [Re PC (Change of Surname) [1997] 2 FLR 730].

- In the case of Re R (Surname: Using Both Parents') [2001] 2 FLR 1358 the Court dealing with a Spanish mother, ordered the use of both the mother's and father's surname as was the custom in Spain.

- The House of Lords has confirmed that when an application is made to change a child's surname the court has to apply the criteria in s.1 and should not make the order unless there is evidence that it would lead to an improvement in the child's welfare.

■ Registration of the name is a relevant, important factor but not 'all important' and does not render irrelevant well recognised considerations which weigh in favour of a child having the same surname as her/his natural father [Dawson v Wearmouth [1999] 1 FLR 1167].

■ A change of forename as opposed to surname is also a very significant matter to be treated with appropriate seriousness e.g. no foster parent or carer should unilaterally change it [Re D, L and LA (Care: Change of Forename) [2003] 1 FLR 339 FD].

NB. In Re J (Specific Issue Orders: Child's Religious Upbringing and Circumcision) 2000 1 FLR, Thorpe LJ and Dame Butler Sloss P in the Court of Appeal agreed there was a small group of important or exceptional decisions which ought not to be taken without the consent of others who have parental responsibility or a court. Case law suggests these include change of surname, medical interventions e.g. circumcision or sterilisation and immunisation against infectious diseases [see Re C [2003] 2FLR 1095] changes of surname [see Re S [2001] 2 FLR 1005] or change of school or type of education [see Re P [2003]1 FLR 286, in which the Court of Appeal emphasised that the courts must not abdicate from their duty to decide such matters where the parents cannot agree. Arguments could also be made based on Article 8(1) that the father's and/or his child's right to respect to family life has been breached by change of the children's surname.

Preference & Entitlements: s.8 Orders

Preference for Child Arrangements Order [s.9 as amended by Sch. 2 para. 4 CFA 2014]

- A court will not grant a Specific Issue or Prohibited Steps Order if a Child Arrangements Order could achieve the same result.

Automatic Entitlement to Apply for Any s.8 Order [s.10 (4) as amended by Sch.3 para.56 ACA 2002 & Sch.2 para. 4 CFA 2014]

- A parent, guardian, special guardian, step parent (which includes a civil partner step parent) who has acquired parental responsibility via s.4A, or a person named in a Child Arrangements Order as someone with whom the child is to live is entitled to apply for any s.8 order.

  NB. The Court of Appeal has confirmed that 'parent' in this context includes an unmarried father [M. v. C. and Calderdale MBC 1992].

Automatic Entitlement to Apply for Child Arrangements Order [s.10 (5) as amended by Sch. 2 para. 4 CFA 2014]

- The following have automatic entitlement to apply for a Child Arrangements Order, or for variation or discharge thereof:

- Any party to a marriage where a child is 'a child of the family' e.g. a stepchild
- Any civil partner in a civil partnership in relation to whom the child is a child of the family
- Anyone with whom the child had been living for a period of 3 years which need not have been continuous but which must have begun not more than 5 years before the making of the application.
- Where a Child Arrangements Order exists (and relates to when and with whom a child is to live) , anyone with the consent of each person named as a person with whom the child is to live
- Anyone with the consent of all who hold parental responsibility (if child is 'in care', this includes the local authority as well as the parents)

Automatic Entitlement of Local Authority Foster Carer to Apply for a Child Arrangements Order [s.10 (5A)]

■ A local authority foster carer is entitled to apply for a Child Arrangements Order (specifying with whom the child shall live and/or when) if the child has lived with her/him for a period of 1 year immediately preceding the application [s.10(5A) introduced by s.113 ACA 2002 and amended by Sch.2 para.5(4) CFA 2014].

Entitlement of a Relative to Apply for Child Arrangements Order [s.10 (5B)]

■ S.10 Children Act 1989 (power of the court to make orders under s.8 of that Act), is amended by the insertion of a s.10(5B) as follows:

- 'A relative of a child is entitled to apply for a Child Arrangements Order (specifying with whom the child shall live and/or when) with respect to the child if the child has lived with the relative for a period of at least 1 year immediately preceding the application'

Entitlement to Seek Court's Leave to Make Application for Any s.8 Order [ss.9 &10 as amended by s.113 & Sch.3 para.56 ACA 2002]

■ The following are entitled to seek the court's leave to make an application for any s.8 Order:

- A child if the court is satisfied s/he has sufficient understanding
- A local authority foster carer if s/he was the foster carer within the last 6 months and has the local authority's consent, is a relative or is eligible because the child has lived with her/him for at least 1 year preceding the application
- Anyone else once the court has considered the criteria set out in s.10 (9)

■ The local authority cannot apply for a Child Arrangements Order nor may one be made in its favour, though it could apply for a Prohibited Steps or

Specific Issue Order for a child being cared for by a parent/other care giver or being 'accommodated'.

- ▨ A court can, in Family Proceedings, make a s.8 Order even if no application has been received [s.10 (1) (b)].

- ▨ Applications by a child are considered to raise issues more appropriate for determination by the High Court and should be transferred there for hearing according to the direction of the then President of High Court Family Division in February 1993.

- ▨ It has been suggested that this direction is in breach of Article 6 (Right to a Fair Trial) and the 'Equality of Arms' principle used by the European Court in such cases.

- ▨ In Re A (Contact: Separate Representation) [2001] 1 FLR 715, Dame Elizabeth Butler-Sloss P, Potter and Hale JJ granted leave to appeal against a County Court judgement that a 4 year old girl whose mother has sought separate representation on the child's behalf by the National Youth Advocacy Service (NYAS) should not be granted it. The Court of Appeal ordered that the child should be represented by the Official Solicitor not NYAS and supported the argument that the decision in the County Court risked there being a breach of this girl's rights under Articles 3, 6, and 8 of the European Convention.

- ▨ It has also been suggested that provision of s.10 (8) restricting children's participation in s.8 proceedings to those cases in which they seek to be made a party is also in breach generally of children's rights to representation, protected by Articles 6, 8 and 14 of the Convention and also a breach of Article 12 UNCRC (see the very important Court of Appeal decision in Mabon v Mabon [2005] 2 FLR 1011).

Criteria for Granting Leave to Make a s.8 Application [s.10 (9)]

■ The court must in deciding whether or not to grant leave, have particular regard to:

- The nature of the proposed application
- The applicant's connection with the child
- Any risk there might be of the proposed application disrupting the child's life to such an extent s/he would be harmed by it, and
- (Where a child is being looked after by a local authority), its plans for her/his future and wishes/feelings of her/his parents

NB. For purposes of seeking leave to make an application, the child's welfare is not the paramount consideration (because s.1 (1) does not apply). Except in an emergency, the interests of justice require notice of application for leave to be given to all parties likely to be affected (see Re M (Prohibited Steps Order: Application for Leave) 1993 1 FLR 275 and Re W (A Child: Contact Leave to Apply) 2000 1 FLR 185].

Application for Variation or Discharge of s.8 Order [s.10]

- The following are entitled to apply for variation or discharge of a s.8 order:

  - Anyone entitled to apply for a s.8 order or who has the leave of the court
  - Any civil partner in a civil partnership in relation to whom the child is a child of the family
  - A parent, guardian, special guardian or any holder of a Child Arrangements Order
  - A person who has parental responsibility by virtue of s.4A

- The following persons may apply for a variation/ discharge of a Child Arrangements Order:

  - Any party to a marriage (whether or not subsisting) where child is a 'child of the family'
  - Any civil partner in a civil partnership in relation to whom the child is a child of the family
  - Any person with whom child has lived for total of 3 years in period 3 months to 5 years prior to application
  - A local authority foster carer if the child has lived with her/him for at least 1 year preceding the application
  - Where a Child Arrangements Order is in force, any person with consent of each person in whose favour that Order exists
  - If child in local authority care, any person with the consent of the local authority, or

- In any other case, with the consent of those (if any) with parental responsibility
- Anyone on whose application a s.8 order was previously made
- A person named in a Child Arrangements Order
- Any person prescribed by rules of court

Special Guardianship [s.14A–G introduced by s.115 ACA 2002]

Purpose of Special Guardianship Orders

- Special Guardianship Orders are intended to meet the needs of children who cannot live with their birth parents, for whom adoption is not appropriate but who could still benefit from a legally secure placement.

- These conditions were found to be met in the case of A Local Authority v Y, Z and Others [2006] Fam Law 448, which is thought to be the first reported case on the making of Special Guardianship Orders.

- In this case, the court determined special guardianship was the most appropriate order where 2 older children from a family of 5 had been placed by the local authority with an aunt and uncle for 2 years and the 3rd child had been placed with another aunt and her partner for almost 2 years. The youngest 2 children had been placed for adoption. The Court emphasised special guardianship would serve the best interests of the 3 older children: it was in accordance with their wishes; they had been with the particular couples for 2 years; had made progress during that time; and the relationships needed cementing. The children (said the Court), required the permanence stability and security that special guardianship would provide; it was preferable to alternatives under the CA 1989; and adoption was neither sought nor desirable.

■ The court also made an order for defined contact with the mother. This case recognises the intended half-way house outcome of special guardianship that confers security for the child as it confers parental responsibility yet preserves the parent/child relationship and can, if required, be varied or discharged.

NB. The following Court of Appeal judgements provide general guidance with respect to 'Adoption Order or Special Guardianship' Re S [2007] 1 FLR 819 CA Thorpe, Tuckey & Wall LJJ; Re AJ [2007] 1 FLR 507 CA Scott Baker & Wall LJJ; Re M-J1 FLR 691 CA Thorpe, Carnwath & Wall LJJ.

Definition & Conditions for Making a Special Guardianship Order [s.14A]

■ A Special Guardianship Order appoints 1 or more individuals as 'special guardian/s' for a child [s.14A (1)].

■ A special guardian must:

- Be aged 18 or over and
- Not be a parent of the child in question [s.14A(2)]

■ The court may make a Special Guardianship Order with respect to any child on the application of an individual (or joint application of more than 1 such individual – couples need not be married) who:

- Is/are entitled to make such an application with respect to the child or
- Has/have obtained leave of the court [s.14A(3)]

■ A person who is, or was at any time within the last 6 months, a local authority foster carer of a child may not apply for a Special Guardianship Order with respect to that child unless s/he has the authority's consent, is a relative or the child has lived with her/him for a total of at least 1 year preceding the application [effect of s.14A (4)].

Eligibility to Make an Application for Special Guardianship Order [s.14A (5)–(7)]

■ The individuals who are entitled to apply for a Special Guardianship Order with respect to a child are:

- Any guardian of the child
- Any individual who is named in a Child Arrangements Order as a person with whom the child is to live
- Any person with whom the child has lived for at least 3 years (in the period 3 months to 5 years before the application is made)
- Where a Child Arrangements Order is in force with respect to the child, any person who has consent of those named in a Child Arrangements Order

- Where the child is in the care of the local authority, any person who has the consent of that authority
- Any person who has the consent of each of those (if any) who have parental responsibility
- A local authority foster carer or a relative with whom the child has lived for a period of at least 1 year immediately preceding the application [s.14A(5) as amended by s.38 C&YPA 2008]

■ The court may also make a Special Guardianship Order with respect to a child in any family proceedings in which a question arises with respect to the welfare of the child if:

- An application for the order has been made by an individual (or more than 1 such individual jointly) who is entitled to or has obtained the court's leave
- The court considers that a Special Guardianship Order should be made even though no such application has been made [s.14A(6)]

■ No individual may make an application under s.14A (3) or (6) unless, s/he has given 3 months written notice of her/his intention to make the application:

- (If the child in question is being looked after by a local authority), to that local authority, or
- Otherwise, to the local authority in whose area the individual is ordinarily resident [s.14A(7)]

Response to Application for Special Guardianship Order [s.14A (8)–(13)]

■ On receipt of such a notice, the local authority must investigate the matter and prepare a report for the court.

■ The court may itself ask a local authority to conduct such an investigation and prepare a report, and the local authority is obliged to do so [s.14A (8); (9)].

 NB. The local authority may make such arrangements as it sees fit for any person to act on its behalf in connection with conducting the investigation or preparing the report [s.14A (10)].

■ The court may not make a Special Guardianship Order unless it has received a report dealing with the matters referred to in s.14A (8) [s.14A (11)].

■ Where a person applies for leave to make an application for a Special Guardianship Order, the court in deciding whether to grant leave must have particular regard to:

 • The nature of the proposed application
 • The applicant's connection with the child
 • Any risk there might be of that proposed application disrupting the child's life to such an extent that s/he would be harmed by it and
 • (Where s/he is looked after by a local authority) the authority's plans for her/his future and the wishes and feelings of the parents [s.14A (12)]

NB. When a Placement Order is in force, no Special Guardianship Order may be made in respect of a child unless an application has been made for an Adoption Order and the applicant for the Special Guardianship Order has obtained the court's leave under s.29 (5) or (if s/he is a guardian of the child) has obtained the court's leave under s.47 (5). If leave has been given, the requirement for 3 months notice in s.14A (7) applications does not apply [effect of s.14A (13)].

Making a Special Guardianship Order [s.14B as amended by Sch.2 para. 8 ACA 2006 & Sch.2 para.24 CFA 2014]

■ Before making a Special Guardianship Order, the court must consider whether, if the order were made:

- A Child Arrangements Order containing contact provision should also be made
- Any s.8 order in force with respect to the child should be varied or discharged
- If a provision contained in a Child Arrangements Order with respect to the child is not discharged, any Enforcement Order relating to that provision should be revoked
- Where an activity direction has been made in proceedings for making, variation or discharge of a Child Arrangements Order or in other proceedings that relate to such an order, that direction should be discharged [s.14B(1) as amended]

■ 'Contact provision' as described in s.14B(1) means provision which regulates arrangements relating to with whom a child is to spend time or otherwise have contact; or when s/he is to spend time or otherwise have contact with any person (other than as a result of living with the person) [s.14B(1A) as inserted by Sch.2 para.25 CFA 2014].

■ On making a Special Guardianship Order, the court may also:

- Give leave for the child to be known by a new surname
- Grant the leave required by s.14C(3)(b), either generally or for specified purposes [s.14B(2)]

Effect of a Special Guardianship Order [s.14C]

■ The effect of a Special Guardianship Order is that while the order remains in force:

- A special guardian appointed by the order has parental responsibility for the child and
- Subject to any other order in force with respect to the child under the Children Act, is entitled to exercise parental responsibility to the exclusion of any other person with parental responsibility for the child (apart from another special guardian) [s.14C(1)]

■ A special guardian is *not* entitled to provide consent to key decisions where statute or case law require the consent of more than 1 person with parental responsibility in a matter affecting the child e.g:

- Sterilisation/circumcision
- Adoption or placement for adoption

- While a Special Guardianship Order is in force with respect to a child, no person may (without either the written consent of every person who has parental responsibility for the child or leave of the court):

  - Cause the child to be known by a new surname or
  - Remove her/him from the UK [s.14C(3)]

  NB. The child's special guardian is allowed to remove the child from the UK for a period of less than 3 months, [s.14C (4)].

- If the child with respect to whom a Special Guardianship Order is in force dies, her/his special guardian must take reasonable steps to give notice of that fact to each:

  - Parent of the child with parental responsibility and
  - Guardian of the child

  NB. If the child has more than 1 special guardian, and 1 has taken such steps in relation to a particular parent or guardian, any other special guardian need not also do so [s.14C (5)].

Variation and Discharge of a Special Guardianship Order [s.14D]

- The court may vary or discharge a Special Guardianship Order on the application of:

- The special guardian (or any of them, if there is more than 1)
- Any parent or guardian of the child concerned
- Any individual who is named in a Child Arrangements Order as a person with whom the child is to live
- Any individual not falling into the above categories, who has, or immediately before the making of the special guardianship order had, parental responsibility for the child
- The child her/himself or
- A local authority designated in a Care Order with respect to the child [s.14D(1)]

■ In any family proceedings in which a question arises with respect to the welfare of a child with respect to whom a Special Guardianship Order is in force, the court may also vary or discharge that order if it considers that it should be varied or discharged, even though no application has been made under s.14D (1) [s.14D (2)].

■ The following must obtain the leave of the court before making an application under s.14D(1):

- The child
- Any parent or guardian of her/him
- Any step-parent who has acquired, and has not lost, parental responsibility for by virtue of s.4A
- Any individual (other than special guardian, parent or guardian or who is named in a Child Arrangements Order) who immediately before the making of the Special Guardianship Order

had, but no longer has, parental responsibility for her/him

- When the person applying for leave to make an application under s.14D(1) is the child, the court may only grant leave if it is satisfied that s/he has sufficient understanding to make the proposed application [s.14D(4)].

- The court may not grant leave to a person (other than the child) under s.14D (3) unless it is satisfied that there has been a significant change in circumstances since the making of the Special Guardianship Order [s.14D (5)].

Special Guardianship Order: Supplementary Provisions [s.14E]

- In proceedings in which any question of making, varying or discharging a Special Guardianship Order arises, the court must (in the light of any rules made by virtue of 14E(3)):

  - Draw up a timetable with a view to determining the question without delay and
  - Give such directions as it considers appropriate for the purpose of ensuring, so far as reasonably practicable, the timetable is adhered to [s.14E(1)]

NB. S.14E (1) applies also in relation to proceedings in which any other question with respect to a Special Guardianship Order arises. A Special Guardianship Order, or an order varying one, may contain provisions which are to have effect for a specified period [s.14E (4)].

Special Guardianship Order Support Services [14F]

▦ Each local authority must make arrangements for the provision within its area of special guardianship support services i.e:

- Counselling, advice and information and
- Such other services as are prescribed [s.14F(1)]

▦ At the request of any of the following persons, a local authority may carry out an assessment of that person's needs for special guardianship support services:

- A child with respect to whom a Special Guardianship Order is in force
- A special guardian
- A parent

▦ A local authority may, at the request of any other person, carry out an assessment of that person's needs for special guardianship support services [s.14F (4)].

▦ Where, as a result of an assessment, a local authority decides that a person has needs for special guardianship support services, it must then decide whether to provide any such services to that person [s.14F(5)]

■ The local authority must prepare a plan in accordance with which special guardianship support services are to be provided to the person and keep the plan under review, *if* the:

- Local authority decides to provide any special guardianship support services to a person, and
- Circumstances fall within a prescribed description [s.14F(6) Children Act 1989]

■ A local authority may provide special guardianship support services (or any part of them) by securing their provision by:

- Another local authority; or
- A person as defined in the Special Guardianship Support Services Regulations 2005

NB. A local authority may also arrange with any such authority or person for that other authority or that person to carry out the local authority's functions in relation to assessments under s.14.

■ A local authority may carry out an assessment of the needs of any person for the purposes of special guardianship at the same time as an assessment of her/his needs is made under any other provision of the Children Act or under any other enactment [s.14F(10) Children Act 1989]

■ S.27 (co-operation between authorities) applies in relation to the exercise of functions of a local authority introduced by s.115 as it applies in relation to the exercise of functions of a local authority under Part 3 [s.14F(11) Children Act 1989].

NB. In R (TT) v London Borough of Merton [2012] EWHC 2055 (Admin) Mr Justice Edwards-Stuart ruled that the borough's payment of only two thirds of its fostering allowance to a special guardian was unlawful.

Special Guardianship Order Support Services: Representations [14G]

▪ Every local authority is obliged to establish a procedure for considering representations (including complaints) made to it by any person to whom it may provide special guardianship support services about the discharge of its functions under s.14 F (1) in relation to her/him [s.14G(1) Children Act 1989 inserted by ACA 2002].

▪ The Children Act 1989 Representations Procedure (England) Regulations 2006 Regulations have been made pursuant to s.14G (2) Children Act 1989 (inserted by ACA 2002), providing for such procedures to be in place in relation to any functions associated with the provision of special guardianship support services (see reg. 5) and imposing under reg. 9(1) a time limit of 1 year on the making of the above representations.

▪ The Regulations go on to provide that a local authority *may* consider any representations outside the time limit if, having regard to all the circumstances, it concludes it would not be reasonable to expect the complainant to have made the representations within it (reg. 9(2)(a); and notwithstanding the delay it is still possible to consider the representations effectively and fairly (reg.(2)(b)).

Family Assistance Order (FAO) [s.16 as amended by Sch.3 para.56 ACA 2002 & s.6 CAA 2006]

- When, in any family proceedings, the court has power to make an order under Part 11 with respect to any child, it may (whether or not it makes such an order) make an order requiring a probation officer or a local authority to make an officer available, to advise, assist and (when appropriate) befriend any person named in the order [s.16(1)].

- The persons who may be named in an FAO are:
  - Any parent or guardian of the child
  - Any person with whom the child is living or who is named in a Child Arrangements Order as a person with whom the child is to live, spend time or otherwise have contact
  - The child her/himself

- No court may make a family assistance order unless it has obtained the consent of every person to be named in the order – other than the child [s.16(3)].

- A FAO may direct the person named in the order or such of the persons named in the order as may be specified in the order, to take such steps as may be so specified with a view to enabling the officer concerned to be kept informed of the address of any person named in the order and to be allowed to visit any such person [s.16(4)].

- If the court makes a FAO with respect to a child and the order is in force at the same time as a Child Arrangements Order containing contact provision it may direct the officer concerned to give advice and assistance as regards establishing, improving and maintaining contact to such of the persons named in the order as may be specified in that order [s.16(4A) inserted by s.6(3) CAA 2006].

- 'Contact provision' here means provision which regulates arrangements relating to with whom the child is to spend time or otherwise have contact, or when a child is to spend time or otherwise have contact with any person [s.16(4B) inserted by Sch.2 para. 27 CFA 2014].

- Unless it specifies a shorter period, a FAO shall have effect for a period of 12 months beginning with the day on which it is made [s.16(5)].

- If the court makes a FAO with respect to a child and the order is to be in force at the same time as a s.8 order made with respect to the child, the FAO may direct the officer concerned to report to the court on such matters relating to the s.8 order as the court may require (including the question whether the s.8 order ought to be varied or discharged) [s.16 (6) as substituted by s.6(5) CAA 2006].

- A FAO cannot be made requiring a local authority to make an officer available unless the local authority agrees or the child lives within its area [s.16(7)].

NB. However, in Re C (Family Assistance Order) 1996 3 FCR 514, in which a Director of Social Services was reluctant to allocate an officer though the child lived within the area, Johnson J considered it would not be appropriate to attach a penal notice to the FAO.

Risk Assessments [s.16A inserted by s.7 CAA 2006]

- S.16A applies to any functions of Cafcass (Welsh family proceedings officers) in connection with:

  - Family proceedings in which the court has power to make an order under Part 11 with respect to a child or in which a question with respect to such an order arises
  - An order made by the court in such proceedings [s.16A(1)]

- If, in carrying out any function to which s.16A applies, a Cafcass (Welsh family proceedings) officer is given cause to suspect that the child concerned is at risk of harm, s/he must:

  - Make a risk assessment in relation to the child, and
  - Provide the risk assessment to the court [s.16A(2)]

- A risk assessment, in relation to a child who is at risk of suffering harm of a particular sort, is an assessment of the risk of that harm being suffered by the child [s.16A(3)].

  NB. The officer must provide her/his assesment to the court whatever its conclusions, and should make clear the factor/s that triggered the decision to undertake it.

PART III: SUPPORT FOR CHILDREN & FAMILIES

Determination of 'Need' – Children Act 1989 [s.17 (10)]

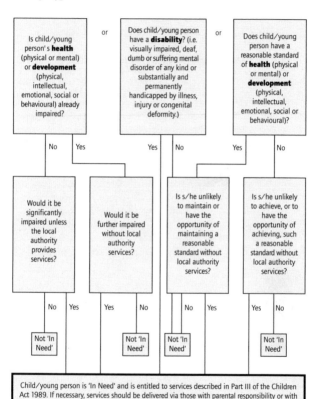

Support for Children & Families

General Duty [s.17 (1)]

- Each local authority has a general duty to safeguard and promote welfare of children 'in need' within its area and, insofar as is consistent with that duty, to promote their upbringing by their families by providing a range and level of services appropriate to their needs.

- For an interpretation of 'within its area', see A v Lambeth CC [2001] 2 FLR 1201 applied also in R on the application of Stewart v Wandsworth London Borough Council [2001] All ER D 8 October 2000.

- In the above case/s, a mother applied for support in respect of children where she lived in Lambeth, in a hostel owned by Hammersmith whilst her children went to school in Wandsworth. It was held that both Lambeth and Wandsworth owed duties to the children.

Definition of Need [s.17 (10); (11)]

- A child is 'in need' if:

    - S/he is unlikely to achieve or maintain, or have opportunity to so do, a reasonable standard of health or development without provision of services by a local authority, or if her/his

- Health or development is likely to be significantly impaired, or further impaired, without such services, or
- S/he is disabled

NB. Health = physical or mental; Development = physical, intellectual, emotional, social or behavioural; Disabled = blind, deaf, dumb or suffering from mental disorder of any kind or substantially and permanently handicapped by illness, injury or congenital deformity, or other such disability as may be prescribed.

Providing Accommodation for Children in Need [s.17 as amended by s.116 ACA 2002]

■ Services provided in the exercise of a local authority's duties under s.17 (6) may include providing accommodation, giving assistance in kind or cash.

■ S.24(1) C&YPA 2008 amended s.17(6) Children Act 1989 (*nature of services which may be provided by a local authority for children in need, their families and others*) so as to omit 'in exceptional circumstances' from the criteria for provision of cash.

NB. The intention was to allow local authorities to exercise a much wider discretion over the circumstances in which they can make cash payments to those caring for children in need e.g. to make regular and continuing payments.

■ Those provided with accommodation under s.17 are *not* 'looked after, so for purposes of s.22 (1) (b) as amended by s.116 ACA 2002 (*general duties toward looked after children*), s.22 duties do *not* apply.

▪ R(H) v Wandsworth London borough council; R (Barhanu) v Hackney London borough Council [2007] EWHC 1082 (Admin) confirmed the correct approach was for a local authority to determine if a child required 'accommodation' or merely 'help with accommodation' *without* having regard to the implications of her/him thereafter becoming a looked after child.

Young Carers' Needs Assessment (England) [s.17ZA–C inserted by s.96 CFA 2014]

▪ A local authority in England must assess whether a young carer (see definition on p.27) within its area has needs for support and if so what those needs are if:

- It appears to the authority that the young carer may have needs for support or
- The authority receives a request from the young carer or her/his parent to assess the young carer's need for support [s.17ZA(1)]

NB. S.17ZA(1) does not apply if the local authority has previously carried out a care-related assessment of the young carer in relation to the same person cared for though an assessment must be carried out if the circumstances of the young carer or person cared for have changed since the last care-related assessment [s.17ZA(4)(5)].

- A care-related assessment means:

  - A young carer's needs assessment or
  - An assessment under s.1 Carers (Recognition and Services) Act 1995, s.1 Carers and Disabled Children Act 2000 or s.4(3) Community Care (Delayed Discharges) Act 2003 [s.17ZA(6)]

- A young carer's needs assessment must include an assessment of whether it is appropriate for the young carer to provide or continue to provide, care for the person in question in the light of her/his own need for support, others needs and wishes [s17ZA(7)].

- A local authority in carrying out a young carer's needs assessment must have regard to the extent to which the young carer is participating in or wishes to participate in education, training or recreation, the extent to which s/he works or wishes to work and must involve the young carer, her/his parents and any person who the young carer or her/his parent request the authority to involve. [s.17ZA (8)(9)].

- The local authority that has carried out a young carer's needs assessment must give a written record to:

  - The young carer
  - Her/his parents and
  - Any person to whom the young carer or parent requests the local authority to give a copy [s.17ZA(10)]

NB. If the person cared for is under 18, the written record must state whether the local authority considers her/him to be a 'child in need' [s.17ZA(11)] and a local authority must take reasonable steps to identify the extent to which there are young carers within its area who have needs for support [s.17ZA(12).

Parent Carers' Needs Assessments (England) [s.17ZD–F inserted by s.97 CFA 2014]

■ A local authority in England must assess whether a parent carer in its area has needs for support and if so what they are if:

- It appears to the authority that the parent carer may have needs for support or it receives a request from the parent carer to assess her/his needs for support and
- The local authority is satisfied that the disabled child care for and the disabled child's family are persons for whom it may provide or arrange for the provision of services under s.17 [s.17ZD(3);(4)]

NB. S.17ZD(1) does not apply if the local authority has previously carried out a care-related assessment of the parent carer in relation to the same disabled child cared for though an assessment must be carried out if the circumstances of the parent carer or disabled child have changed since the last care-related assessment [s.17ZD(6);(7)].

- A care-related assessment means:

  - A parent carer's needs assessment or
  - An assessment under s.1 Carers (Recognition and Services) Act 1995, s.6 Carers and Disabled Children Act 2000 or s.4(3) Community Care (Delayed Discharges) Act 2003 [s.17ZA(6)]

- A parent carer's needs assessment must include an assessment of whether it is appropriate for the parent carer to provide or continue to provide care for the disabled child, in the light of the parent carers' needs for support, other needs and wishes [s.17ZD(9)].

- A local authority in carrying out a parent carer's needs assessment must have regard to well-being of the parent carer, the need to safeguard and promote the welfare of the disabled child cared for and other child for whom the parent carer has parental responsibility; and must involve the carer, child for whom the carer has parental responsibility and any person who the parent carer requests the authority to involve [s.17D(10)-(12)].

- A local authority that has carried out a parent carer's needs assessment must give a written record of the assessment to:

  - The parent carer
  - Any person to whom the parent carer requests the authority give a copy [s.17D(13)]

- A local authority in England must take reasonable steps to identify the extent to which there are parent

carers in its area who have needs for support [.
s17D(14).

Inter-Agency Co-operation [s.27]

■ A mutual obligation exists for local authorities to
assist one another unless this is in conflict with their
own statutory duties (see R on application of Stewart
v Wandsworth cited above).

Day Care [s.18]

■ A local authority must provide such day care for pre-
school children aged 5 and under 'in need' and care
and supervised activities for school children 'in need'
within its area outside school hours and in holidays
as is appropriate.

*NB. The meaning of 'appropriate' was considered in
the case of R v London Borough of Brent ex parte B
1994 1 FLR 592.*

■ In so doing the local authority must have regard to
racial groups to which such children belong [Sch.2
para.11].

■ The Children Act 2004 revoked previous duties to
produce a number of plans including the 'early years
development and child care partnership plan' and
introduced an obligation to produce a triennial
strategic 'children and young people's' plan to be
updated annually [s.17 Children Act 2004].

Domiciliary Support [Sch.2 para.8]

■ The local authority is empowered to provide advice, guidance, counselling; occupational, social, cultural or recreational activities; home helps (including laundry facilities) and travel subsidies to access other support services and assistance with holidays.

Direct Payments & Vouchers [s.17A & 17B introduced by s.7 Carers and Disabled Children Act 2000]

■ Instead of itself providing s.17, the local authority may make direct payments to enable the purchase of required service/s for under 18s and who have a disability, to:

- Those who have parental responsibility for the child or
- Directly to a young person aged 16 or 17

NB. Vouchers expressed in terms of time, money or period of short-break services may also be issued to a person with parental responsibility.

Reduction of Need for Care Proceedings etc. [Sch.2 para.7]

■ The local authority must take reasonable steps to:

- Reduce care/criminal/family proceedings leading to care
- Avoid need for secure accommodation
- Encourage children not to commit crime

Prevention of Neglect & Abuse [Sch.2 para.4]

■ The local authority must take reasonable steps through provision of family support services to prevent children within its area suffering ill treatment or neglect.

■ The local authority must inform any other local authority if a child likely to suffer harm lives, or proposes to live in its area.

Accommodation to Protect Child [Sch. 2 para.5]

■ If it appears to it, that a child living on particular premises is suffering or is likely to suffer ill treatment at the hands of another person living there, and that other person proposes to move out, the local authority may assist her/him to obtain alternative accommodation.

Family Centres [Sch.2 para.9]

■ The local authority may also provide in family centres, advice, counselling, recreational activities etc. and accommodation for children, parents, those with parental responsibility and those with whom child is living.

General Duty to Accommodate [s.20 (1)]

■ The local authority must provide accommodation for a child for whom nobody has parental responsibility or who is lost or when, for any reason, the ordinary caregiver is prevented from providing suitable accommodation or care.

NB. Determination of age is often a challenge for unaccompanied asylum seekers. 'A v Croydon London Borough Council: Secretary of State for the Home Department Interested Party;WK v Secretary of State for the Home Department etc [2009] EWHC 939(Admin)' confirmed that there is no reliable means to determine age. An authority's decision made by properly trained and experienced social workers in accordance with guidelines approved by Stanley Burnton J in R (B) v London Borough of Merton [2003] EWHC 1889 (Admin) 2 FLR 888 and taking account of any medical reports (which local authorities are not obliged to seek – see R (A) v London Borough of Croydon [2008] EWHC 2921(Admin)) can be sufficient. However, the Supreme Court 26 November 2009 [2010] 1 FLR (forthcoming) on appeal overturned the decisions of the lower Courts and concluded that whether a person was a child or not was question of fact to be determined on the evidence by a court rather than other kinds of decision makers.

Duty to Accommodate Certain Young People Aged 16–17 inc. [s.20 (3)]

■ The local authority must provide accommodation to children 'in need' in this age group if their welfare would otherwise be 'seriously prejudiced'.

NB. This duty may be enforceable [Re T (Accommodation by Local Authority) [1995] 1 FLR 159].

Power to Accommodate Young Persons 16–20 years inc. [s.20 (5)]

■ A local authority may provide accommodation in any community home which accepts those 16 or over, if it considers it would safeguard or promote the young person's welfare.

NB. R (on the application of G) (FC) (Appellant) v London Borough of Southwark (Respondents) [2009] UKHL 26 judged that 'local authorities should presume any lone, homeless children should be provided with accommodation under s.20 Children Act 1989. Where the criteria for s.20 have been met, children's services do not have the discretion to choose to use s. 17 powers instead to provide accommodation'.

Removal from Accommodation [s.20 (7) as amended by Sch.3 para.59 ACA 2002 & Sch.2 para.28 CFA 2014]

■ Anyone with parental responsibility may remove a child unless s/he is 16 or 17 and disagrees.

■ Effective agreements with parents should reduce potential problems but if 'significant harm' appears likely, emergency protection measures are available.

NB. A person named in a Child Arrangements Order as a person with whom the child is to live or a special guardian can authorise retention of a child in accommodation in spite of a parent's wishes to remove her/him [s.20(9)(a) as amended].

Other Obligations to Accommodate [s.21]

◼ When asked, a local authority must accommodate a child:

- Removed from home on an Emergency Protection or Child Assessment Order
- Subject of Police Powers of Protection
- Remanded (allows detention of child)
- Detained under Police & Criminal Evidence Act 1984
- On a 'Supervision Order' with residence requirements under Children & Young Persons Act 1969 [s.12 AA]

Local Authority Duties toward Looked After Children [ss.22 & Sch.2 para.19A]

◼ Safeguard and promote welfare and make reasonable efforts to allow child access to ordinary services as though still at home [s.22 (3)].

NB. Potentially, the above is a very onerous duty of care owed both to safeguard and promote the child's welfare. There also exists the common law duty of care owed by the local authority to children being looked after under a care order or those who are being accommodated by the local authority.

Even before the decision in Z v UK [2001] 2 FLR 612 (the old X v Bedfordshire CC [1995] 2 FLR 276 case when heard in the English Courts), it had been determined in Barrett v London Borough Council of Enfield [1999] 2 FLR 426 that the local authority owed a common law duty of care towards children in its care. See also for the duty of care in respect of particular decisions taken by individual social workers W v Essex County Council [2000] 1 FLR 657, where the Court of Appeal had held by a majority that a local authority may be liable in negligence and in negligent mis-statement in relation to specific statements made on its behalf by a social worker to prospective foster parents. The foster parents in W alleged that a teenager had been placed with them contrary to specific reassurances given to them by the social worker that no adolescent known or suspected to be a child sexual abuser would be fostered with them. The teenager who was placed with them had in fact been cautioned for indecent assault, which was known to the local authority social worker and then after placement went on to sexually abuse the foster parent's 4 children who then suffered psychiatric illnesses as a result of the trauma. In this case, which was decided before Z (see above) the majority of the Court of Appeal held that the case was distinguishable from X v Bedfordshire County Council in that this case involved harm caused by a child in care to the family in which he was placed. The Court of Appeal, however, did not allow the parents' case to proceed. The appeal to the House of Lords by the parents was allowed and the House reversed the decision, in that they allowed the parents as well as the children, to lodge their claim that they had also suffered as a result of the actions of Social Services.

See also the decision in F v Lambeth London Borough Council [2002] 1 FLR 217 where in this case 2 boys suffered serious harm whilst in the care of the local authority, which had failed to place them with foster parents and had also failed to facilitate contact between the boys and their family. Thus the local authority was held liable in damages for breach of duty of care and for breach of particular sections of the CA 1989 e.g. s22(3), (4),and (5) and s23(7),with Munby J. taking the unusual step of giving judgement in open court so that the failures of the local authority could be noted by the Press.

And see C v Flintshire County Council [2001] 2 FLR 33 where a girl, who had been the subject of a care order due to parental abuse, was seriously bullied and abused whilst in care, and again recovered damages for injuries sustained as a result of the breach of the duty of care.

See also A and B v Essex County Council [2003] 1 FLR 615 where Munby J held that where social workers from Essex Social Services had failed to pass on information about a boy's serious behavioural difficulties (which included being very violent towards his sister who had been placed with the same prospective adoptive parents) to the prospective adoptive parents, then the social workers had failed in their common law duty of care in that they had not provided all the relevant information about the children to A and B and so Essex CC was vicariously liable for any breaches of care established. However, once the prospective adoptive parents continued with the placement after they were fully aware of all the circumstances then at that point the authority's negligence had run its course and no further liability for subsequent problems could arise. Damage sustained after the adoption was not therefore caused by the authority's breach of duty.

NB. In A and S (Children) v Lancashire County Council [2012] EWHC 1689 Mr Justice Peter Jackson found Lancashire County Council liable for the degrading treatment, including physical assault suffered by two brothers who had spent nearly all their lives in care.

- ◼ Endeavour, unless not reasonably practical or consistent with welfare, to promote contact between child and

  - • Parents, and anyone else who has parental responsibility. This duty on the local authority to promote contact was found to have been breached in F v Lambeth London Borough Council [2002] 1 FLR 217 (see above).
  - • Relatives, friends or persons connected with her/ him.

■ Take reasonable steps to keep parents and those who hold parental responsibility informed of child's location.

■ Not to place a child with a disability in unsuitable accommodation.

■ Consult child (according to age and understanding), parent/s, those with parental responsibility and other 'relevant' people [s.22 (4); (5) – found to have been breached in F v Lambeth London Borough Council [2002] 1 FLR 217 (see above)].

NB. In deciding to remove a child from a foster carer, the local authority must consult her/him as well as any children's guardian who has been involved [R v Hereford and Worcester County Council ex parte D [1992] 1 FLR 448].

■ Before making any decision, consider child's race, culture, religion and linguistic background.

NB. The local authority may act contrary to the above in order to protect the public from serious injury.

■ So far as is practicable and consistent with welfare, place a child with parents, or someone with parental responsibility (for a child 'in care' with any previous person named in a Child Arrangements Order as a person with whom the child was to live), relatives or friends or other person connected with child [s.22C(3) & 23(4)-(6) as amended].

NB. Failure to consider, consult and record compliance with such duties will give rise to allegations of a breach of Article 8(1) of the Convention. Thus in Re M [2001] 2 FLR 1300 the local authority had failed to involve the parents in a permanency planning meeting being held on in respect of their child T who had originally been made the subject of a Care Order as a result of failings in both parents who had a history of drug and alcohol abuse. Whilst still on the Care Order T had returned to live with her mother but then had to be removed from her care when the mother was taken into hospital following drug and alcohol poisoning. Shortly after this the local authority decided to and held a meeting to discuss T's future care, including potential adoption if placement with the maternal grandmother did not prove viable. Because of various problems they failed to invite either the parents or their solicitors with whom the local authority had been in contact. Holman J held that the local authority had been in breach of the requirements of Article 8 ECHR taken together with s.6 HRA 1998. Thus the decision of the planning meeting was unlawful and would be quashed. Further, the very fundamental change of plan being put forward by the local authority also breached the parents' rights under Art 8 and the Court ordered that everything should be reviewed at a later full hearing in court where the court would determine what should happen and would also deal with specific applications for the discharge of the Care Order.

■ Advise, assist and befriend the child with a view to promoting her/his welfare when s/he ceases to be looked after [Sch.2 para.19A introduced by s.1 Children (Leaving Care) Act 2000].

Promotion of Educational Achievement of Looked After Children [s.22 (3B) & (3C) inserted by s.99 CFA 2014]

■ A local authority must appoint at least one person for the purposes of discharging the duty imposed by s.22 (3A) (promotion of educational achievement for looked after children) and a person appointed must be an officer employed by that authority or another local authority in England.].

NB. The role envisaged here is often referred to as a 'virtual school head'. Statutory guidance 'Promoting the Education of Looked After Children' July 2014 is available at www.gov.uk/government/publications

Provision of Accommodation & Maintenance for Children Looked After by a Local Authority [s.23 substituted by s.8(1) C&YPA 2008]

- By virtue of s.8(1) C&YPA 2008, s.23 is substituted as follows by:

  - *Provision of accommodation for children in care*: when a child is in the care of a local authority, it is its duty to provide her/him with accommodation [s.22A Children Act 1989]
  - *Maintenance of looked after children*: it is the duty of a local authority to maintain a child it is looking after in other respects apart from the provision of accommodation [s.22B]

- S.22C *(ways in which looked after children are to be accommodated and maintained)* applies as follows when a local authority is looking after a child C [s.22C (1)].

- The local authority must make arrangements for C to live with a person who falls within s.22C (3) (but subject to s.22C(4)) [s.22C(2)].

- A person (P) falls within subsection 22C(3) if:

  - P is a parent of C
  - P is *not* a parent of C but has parental responsibility for her/him; or

- In a case when C is in the care of the local authority and there was a Child Arrangements Order in force with respect her/him immediately before the Care Order was made, P was a named in that order as a person with whom C was to live [s.22C(3)]

NB. S.22C(2) does not require the local authority to make arrangements of the kind mentioned in that subsection if doing so would not be consistent with C's welfare or would not be reasonably practicable [s.22C(4)].

- If the local authority is unable to make arrangements under s.22C (2), it must place C in the placement which is, in its opinion, the most appropriate placement available [s.22C(5)].

- In s.22C(5) 'placement' means placement:

  - With an individual who is a relative, friend or other person connected with C and who is also a local authority foster parent
  - With a local authority foster parent who does not fall within the above category
  - In a children's home in respect of which a person is registered under Part 2 Care Standards Act 2000; or
  - (Subject to s.22D), placement in accordance with other arrangements which comply with any regulations made for the purposes of s.22 [s.22C(6)]

■ In determining the most appropriate placement for C, the local authority must, subject to s.22(9B) and other provisions of this Part (in particular, duties under s.22 Children Act 1989):

- Give preference to a placement falling within the first paragraph in s.22C(6) above over placements falling within the other 3 paragraphs of that section
- Comply, so far as is reasonably practicable in all the circumstances of C's case, with the requirements of s.22C(8) and
- Comply with s.22C(9) unless that is not reasonably practicable [s.22C(7)]

■ The local authority must ensure the placement is such that:

- It allows C to live near C's home
- It does not disrupt C's education or training
- If C has a sibling for whom the local authority is also providing accommodation, it enables C and the sibling to live together
- If C is disabled, the accommodation provided is suitable to C's particular needs [s.22C(8)]

■ The placement must be such that C is provided with accommodation within the local authority's area [s.22C (9)].

■ The local authority may determine the terms:

- Of any arrangements its makes under s.22C(2) in relation to C (including terms as to payment); and
- On which it places C with a local authority foster parent (including terms as to payment but subject to any order made under s.49 Children Act 2004) [s.22C(10)]

NB. The appropriate national authority may make regulations for, and in connection with, the purposes of s.22 [s.22C (11) Children Act 1989].

■ 22D *(review of child's case before making alternative arrangements for accommodation)* provides that:

- When a local authority is providing accommodation for a child (C) other than by arrangements under s.22C(6)(d), it must not make such arrangements for her/him unless it has decided to do so in consequence of a review of C's case carried out in accordance with regulations made under s.26 Children Act 1989

NB. S.22D(1) does not prevent a local authority making arrangements for C under s.22C(6)(d) if it is satisfied that in order to safeguard her/his welfare it is necessary to make such arrangements and to do so as a matter of urgency [s.22D(2).

■ 22E *(children's homes provided by appropriate national authority)* provides that:

- When a local authority place a child it is looking after in a children's home provided, equipped and maintained by an appropriate national authority under s.82(5), it must do so on such terms as that national authority may from time to time determine

■ 22F *(regulations as to children looked after by local authorities)* provides that Part 2 of Sch.2 has effect for the purposes of making further provision as to children looked after by local authorities and in particular as to the regulations which may be made under s.22C(11).

■ Schedule 1 (which makes amendments supplementary to, and consequential on, the provisions of s.22 including a power to make regulations about an 'independent review mechanism' for certain decisions in relation to foster parents) has effect [s.8 (2)].

General Duty of Local Authority to Secure Sufficient Accommodation [s.22G inserted by s.9 C&YPA 2008]

- ■ S.9 inserts after s.22F Children Act 1989 (inserted by s.8), a s.22G *(general duty of local authority to secure sufficient accommodation for looked after children)* as follows:

  - It is the general duty of a local authority to take steps that secure, so far as reasonably practicable, the outcome in s.22G(2) [s.22G(1) Children Act 1989]
  - The outcome is that the local authority is able to provide the children mentioned in s.22G(3) with accommodation that is within the authority's area; and meets the needs of those children [s.22G(2) Children Act 1989]

- ■ The children referred to in s.22G(2) are those:

  - The local authority is looking after
  - In respect of whom the authority is unable to make arrangements under s.22C(2), and
  - Whose circumstances are such that it would be consistent with their welfare for them to be provided with accommodation that is in the authority's area [s.22G(3) Children Act 1989]

- ■ In taking steps to secure the outcome in s.22G(2), the local authority must have regard to the benefit of having:

- A number of accommodation providers in its area that is, in its opinion, sufficient to secure that outcome and
- A range of accommodation in its area capable of meeting different needs that is, in its opinion, sufficient to secure that outcome [s.22G(4) Children Act 1989]

Visits to Children Looked After by a Local Authority [s.23ZA introduced by s.15 C&YPA 2008]

- S.15 C&PA 2008 introduced a s.23ZA to the Children Act 1989 which applies to a:
  - Child looked after by a local authority
  - A child or young person who was looked after but who has ceased to be looked after by it as a result of prescribed circumstances [s.23ZA(1)]

- It is the duty of the local authority to:
  - Ensure that a person to whom s.23 applies is visited by a 'representative' of the authority
  - Arrange for appropriate advice, support and assistance to be available to a person to whom s.23 applies who seeks it from that local authority [s.23ZA(2) inserted by s.13]

- The duties imposed by s.23ZA(2) are to be discharged in accordance with any regulations made for the purposes of this section by the appropriate national authority (in England the Care Planning, Placement & Case Review (England) Regulations 2010) and are subject to any requirement imposed by or under an enactment applicable to the place in which the person to whom this section applies is accommodated e.g. in custody or detained under the Mental Health Act [s.23ZA(3)].

■ Regulations under s.23 for the purposes of the above regulations make provision about the:

- Frequency of visits
- Circumstances in which a person to whom this section applies must be visited by a representative and
- Functions of a representative [s.23ZA(4)]

■ In choosing a representative a local authority must satisfy themselves that the person chosen has the necessary skills and experience to perform the functions of a representative [s.23ZA(5)].

NB. 'Appropriate national authority' means in England the Secretary of State and in Wales the Welsh Ministers [s.23ZA(6)]. CAE's guide to Fostering includes a comprehensive summary of the relevant regulations.

Independent Visitors for Children Looked After by a Local Authority [s.16]

■ S.16 inserts a new s.23ZB into the 1989 Act and requires that a local authority looking after a child to appoint an independent person to be the child's visitor if:

- The child falls within a description prescribed in regulations made by the appropriate national authority or
- In any other case, it appears to the local authority that it would be in the child's interests to do so [s.23ZB(1)]

NB. Thus, the group for whom independent visitors must be appointed is extended and previous provisions in para. 2 of Sch.17 Children Act 1989 are abolished.

■ A person appointed under s.23 must visit, befriend and advise the child [s.23ZB (2)].

■ A person appointed under s.23 is entitled to recover from the appointing authority any reasonable expenses incurred by that person for the purposes of that person's functions under s.23 [s.23ZB(3)].

■ A person's appointment as a visitor in pursuance of this s.23 comes to an end if the:

- Child ceases to be looked after by the local authority
- Person resigns the appointment by giving notice in writing to the appointing authority or
- Authority gives notice in writing that it has terminated it [s.23ZB(4)]

■ The ending of such an appointment does not affect any duty under this s.23 to make a further appointment [s.23ZB (5)].

■ If a local authority propose to appoint a visitor for a child under s.23, the appointment shall not be made if the:

- Child objects to it and
- Authority is satisfied s/he has sufficient understanding to make an informed decision [s.23ZB(6)]

■ If a visitor has been appointed for a child under s.23 the local authority must terminate the appointment if the:

- Child objects to its continuing; and
- Authority is satisfied that the child has sufficient understanding to make an informed decision [s.23ZB(7)]

■ If the local authority give effect to a child's objection under s.23ZB(6) or (7) and the objection is to having anyone as the child's visitor, the authority does not have to propose to appoint another person under s.23ZB(1) until the objection is withdrawn [s.23ZB(8)].

NB. The appropriate national authority (in England the Secretary of State; in Wales the Welsh Ministers) have the power to make regulations as to circumstances in which a person is to be regarded for the purposes of s.23 as 'independent' of the appointing authority [s.23ZB (9);(10)].

Review Duties [s.26 as amended by s.118 ACA 2002]

■ Each local authority, for a child in its care must:

- Keep her/his s.31A plan under review and if it is of the opinion that some change is required, to revise it and make a new plan
- Consider whether an application should be made to discharge the Care Order (found to have been breached in F v Lambeth London Borough Council [2002] 1 FLR 217 – see above)

■ A local authority which is 'providing accommodation' for a child i.e. one who is not subject of a Care Order, must:

- If there is no plan for her/his future, prepare one
- If there is such a plan, keep it under review and if of the opinion that some change is required, to revise the plan or make a new one (found to have been breached in F v Lambeth London Borough Council [2002] 1 FLR 217 -see above)

Appointment & Functions of Independent Reviewing Officers (IROs) [s.25A–C inserted by s.10(1) C&YPA 2008]

■ s.10(1) inserts, after s.25 Children Act 1989 a s.25A (*appointment of independent reviewing officer*) and means that:

- If a local authority is looking after a child, it must appoint an individual as the independent reviewing officer (IRO) for that child's case
- The initial appointment under s.25A(1) must be made before the child's case is first reviewed in accordance with regulations made under s.26
- If a vacancy arises in respect of a child's case, the local authority must make another appointment under s.25A (1) as soon as is practicable.
- An appointee must be of a description prescribed in regulations made by the appropriate national authority [s.25A]

■ s.10(1) further inserts a s.25B (*functions of the independent reviewing officer*) and means that:

- The IRO must monitor the performance by the local authority of its functions in relation to the child's case, participate, in accordance with regulations made by the appropriate national authority in any review of the child's case, ensure that any ascertained wishes and feelings of the child concerning the case are given due consideration by the local authority, and perform any other function which is prescribed in regulations made by the appropriate national authority [s.25B(1)]

NB. The duty to monitor local authority performance with respect to the 'case' is wider than the previous IRO role which was limited to the review functions.

- An IRO's functions must be performed in such manner (if any) as may be prescribed in regulations made by the appropriate national authority and having regard to such guidance as that authority may issue in relation to the discharge of those functions [s.25B(2)]
- If the IRO considers it appropriate to do so, the child's case may be referred by that officer to an officer of the Children and Family Court Advisory and Support Service (Cafcass) or a Welsh family proceedings officer [s.25B(3)]

■ If the IRO is not an officer of the local authority, it is the duty of the authority to co-operate with that individual and to take all such reasonable steps as that individual may require of them to enable that individual's functions under s.25B to be performed satisfactorily [s.25B(4)]

■ s.10(1) also inserts a s.25C (*referred cases*) and:

- Means that in relation to children whose cases are referred to officers under s.25B(3), the Lord Chancellor may by regulations extend any functions of the officers in respect of family proceedings (within the meaning of s.12 of the Criminal Justice and Court Services Act 2000) to other proceedings
- Requires any functions of the officers to be performed in the manner prescribed by regulations

NB. The Care Planning, Placement & Case Review (England) Regulations cover reviews and IROs. They are comprehensively summarised in CAE's guide to Fostering. The power to make regulations in s.25C Children Act 1989 is exercisable in relation to functions of Welsh family proceedings officers only with the consent of the Welsh Ministers [s.25C(2) introduced by s.10(1)].

General Duties toward Persons 'Qualifying for Advice and Assistance' [s.24 substituted by s.4 Children (Leaving Care) Act 2000 and amended by Sch.3 paras. 60 & 61 ACA 2002]

■ A person 'qualifying for advice and assistance' is now defined as a person:

- Aged 16 or over but under 21
- With respect to whom a Special Guardianship Order is in force (or was before s/he reached 18 years of age) and
- Who was, immediately before the making of that order, looked after by a local authority or
- Is under 21 and
- At any time between being 16 and before being 18 was looked after, accommodated or fostered

NB. Looked after, accommodated or fostered means here looked after by a local authority, accommodated by or on behalf of a voluntary organisation, accommodated in a private children's home or accommodated for a consecutive minimum period of 3 months by any health or special health authority, primary care trusts (now re-badged clinical commissioning groups CCGs) or local education authority or in any care home, independent hospital or any accommodation provided by a NHS trust or privately fostered.

■ In the case of a person looked after by a local authority, the duty falls to the last local authority which looked after her/him, to take such steps as it thinks necessary to discharge duties under s.24(1A) and s.24(1B) – described below.

■ For purposes of duties and powers in s.24 (general advice/assistance or associated with education/ training/employment) the relevant local authority is:

- In the case of a person who was looked after, the local authority which last looked after her/him
- In any other case, the local authority within whose area person is (if s/he has asked for help of a sort which can be provided under s.24A or s.24B)

■ The relevant local authority must first decide:

- If a person qualifying for advice and assistance needs it and
- Where the person was not being looked after by a local authority, be satisfied whoever had been doing so does not have the necessary facilities

■ If the above 2 conditions are met, the local authority *must* advise and befriend the person if s/he was being looked after by a local authority or accommodated by or on behalf of a voluntary organisation, and *may* do so in any other case [s.24A (1)–(4) as amended by Children (Leaving Care) Act 2000 and Sch.3 paras.61 & 62 ACA 2002].

NB. When the local authority is thus obliged or empowered, it may also provide assistance in kind and in exceptional circumstances assistance may be given by providing accommodation (if assistance can't be provided by virtue of s.24B), or in cash [s.24A (4)–(5) as amended by Children (Leaving Care) Act 2000 and s.116 ACA 2002].

■ The relevant local authority may give assistance to a person who 'qualifies for advice and assistance' by contributing to expenses incurred by her/him living near the place where s/he is working/seeking work [s.24B(1) as amended by Children (Leaving Care) Act 2000 and Sch.3 para.62 ACA 2002].

■ The relevant local authority may also give assistance to a person aged under 24 and does (or would, if under 21) qualify for advice and assistance by:

- Contributing to expenses incurred by the person living near the place s/he is or will be receiving education/training or
- Making a grant to enable her/him meet expenses connected to education/training [s.24B(2);(3) as amended by Children (Leaving Care) Act 2000]

NB. Where assisting a person with education/ training, the local authority may disregard interruptions of attendance if the course is resumed as soon as reasonably practicable.

■ When the local authority is satisfied a person entitled to advice and assistance described above and in full-time further (i.e. full-time residential) or higher education, needs vacation accommodation, it must assist by:

- Providing suitable accommodation or
- Paying the person enough to enable her/him to secure such accommodation [s.24B(5) as amended by Children (Leaving Care) Act 2000]

NB. See the leaving care section below for more detail on this support including the Higher Education bursary.

Additional Duties to 'Eligible', 'Relevant' & 'Former Relevant' Children [s. 22; s.23A–C; Sch.2 paras. 19B –19C; as amended/ introduced by Children (Leaving Care) Act 2000]

■ The local authority has additional responsibilities for explicitly defined groups of 16 and 17 year olds who are, or who have been looked after as well as to those aged 18 or over defined as having belonged to one of those groups [see Leaving Care section below].

Leaving Care: Summary

Children (Leaving Care) Act 2000, Care Planning, Placement and Case Review (England) Regulations 2010 & Care Leavers (England) Regulations 2010

■ A summary of these provisions is that they:

- Place a duty on local authorities to assess the needs of 'eligible' and 'relevant' children
- Define 'eligible' children as those aged 16 or 17 who have been looked after for a period of 13 weeks continuously or in aggregate (with any period before age 14 excluded for purpose of aggregation)
- Define 'relevant' children as eligible young people of 16 or 17 who cease to be looked after with an additional category of those detained at the age of 16 in a Young Offender Institute (YOI), Secure Training Centre (STC), local authority secure children's home (LASCH) or hospital (those returning home for 6 months or more or in receipt of short-breaks of up to 4 weeks are excluded)
- Clarify that the 'responsible local authority' will be the one which last looked after the child
- Introduce a duty on the responsible local authority to keep in touch with all qualifying care leavers
- Oblige local authorities to formulate for all eligible and relevant children (potentially up to 25 years of age) regularly reviewed 'pathway

plans' (replacing care plans), which cover education, training, career plan and the support needed

- Introduce 'personal advisers' (PAs) for each eligible, relevant or former relevant child to help draw up and support pathway plans and keep in touch with individuals
- Oblige local authorities in relevant cases, to assist care leavers in higher education with vacation accommodation
- Empower responsible local authorities to assist with costs of education and training up to age of twenty five, whenever a course may commence
- Place local authorities under a duty to financially support care leavers and remove entitlement from specified means-tested benefits from eligible and relevant young people.

Eligible Child: Local Authority Duties

■ A young person is *eligible* for after care if s/he:

  • Is aged 16 or 17 and
  • Has been looked after by a local authority for a period/s totalling 13 weeks which began after s/he was 14 years old and ended when s/he had reached 16 years of age [Sch.2 para. 19B(2) CA 1989 and reg.40(1) CPP& CR Regs.2010]]

■ In spite of meeting the above criteria, the child is *not* eligible for this service if:

  • The local authority had arranged to place an accommodated child in a pre-planned series of short-break placements each intended to last no more than 17 days, and not exceeding 75 days in total in any period of 12 months and
  • At the end of each placement, the child returned to the care of a parent or a person with parental responsibility [para.19B(2) Children Act 1989 and reg.40(2) Care Planning, Placement & Case Review (England) Regulations 2010].

■ If s/he *is* an eligible child, the responsible authority must assess her/his needs in accordance with reg.42 CPP&CR Regs.2010 below so as to determine what advice, assistance and support it would be appropriate to provide under the Children (Leaving Care) Act 2000. Based upon the above assessment, the local authority must then prepare a pathway plan for her/him [s.1 (4) Children (Leaving Care) Act 2000 and reg.41 CPP&CR Regs.2010].

■ When carrying out the assessment of the child's needs in accordance with para.19B (4), the local authority must determine whether it would be appropriate to provide advice, assistance and support in order to facilitate a 'staying put arrangement' and with a view to maintaining such an arrangement after the local authority ceases to look after her/him [Sch.2 para.19BA (2) inserted by s.98(3) CFA 2014].

■ The local authority must provide advice, assistance and support in order to facilitate a staying put arrangement if its assessment of need indicates that it would be appropriate to do so and the eligible child and local authority foster parent wish to make a staying put arrangement [Sch.2. para.19B (3) inserted by s.98(3) CFA 2014].

Eligible Child: Assessment of Needs for Purposes of Formulating a Pathway Plan [Reg.42 Care Planning, Placement & Case Review (England) Regulations 2010]

■ The responsible authority must complete the assessment of a child's needs in accordance with para.19B(4) of Sch.2 Children Act 1989 not more than 3 months after the date on which s/he reaches the age of 16 or becomes an eligible child after that age [reg.42(1)].

■ In carrying out its assessment of the young person's likely needs when it ceases to look after her/him, the responsible authority must take account of the following considerations about her/him:

- State of health (including physical, emotional and mental health) and development
- Continuing need for education, training or employment
- Support that will be available to her/him from parents and other connected persons
- Actual and anticipated financial resources and capacity to manage personal finances independently
- The extent to which s/he possesses the practical and other skills necessary for independent living
- Needs for continuing needs for care, support and accommodation
- Her/his wishes and feelings and those of any parent of her/his and any person who is not a parent but who has parental responsibility for her/him and the 'appropriate person'
- The views of any person or educational institution that provides the child with education or training (and if s/he has a statement of special educational needs, the local authority that maintains the statement), the IRO, any person providing health (physical, mental or emotional health) or dental care or treatment to the child, the personal adviser appointed for her/him, and any other person whose views the

responsible authority or the child consider may be relevant [reg.42(2) CPP & CR Regs.2010]

Eligible Child: Pathway Plan [Reg.43 CPP&CR Regulations 2010]

- A *pathway plan* must be prepared as soon as possible after the assessment of the child's needs and must include, in particular her/his care plan and the following information referred to in Sch.8 of the CPP& CR regulations:

  - Name of the child's PA
  - Nature and level of contact and personal support to be provided to the child, and by whom
  - Details of the accommodation the child is to occupy when s/he ceases to be looked after
  - Plan for the child's continuing education or training when s/he ceases to be looked after
  - How the responsible authority will assist the child in obtaining employment or other purposeful activity or occupation
  - Support to be provided to enable her/him to develop and sustain appropriate family and social relationships
  - A programme to develop the practical and other skills s/he needs to live independently
  - Financial support to be provided to enable the child to meet her/his accommodation and maintenance costs
  - The child's health care needs, including any physical, emotional or mental health needs and

how they are to be met when s/he ceases to be looked after.

- Responsible authority's contingency plans for action to be taken in the event that the pathway plan ceases to be effective for any reason [reg.43(1) & Sch.8 CPP& CR Regs.2010]

- The pathway plan must, in relation to each of the matters referred to in Sch.8 above set out the:

  - Manner in which the responsible authority proposes to meet C's needs, and
  - Date by which, and by whom, any action required to implement any aspect of the plan will be carried out [reg.43(2)]

NB. Failure to involve a child of 16 or over will be a breach of Article 6 of the European Convention – see Re M (Care Challenging Decisions by Local Authority) [2001] 2 FLR 1300 in which a failure to involve the parents of a child in a permanency planning meeting was regarded as such.

Eligible Child: Functions of the Personal Adviser (PA) [Sch.2 para. 19C Children Act 1989 & Reg.44 CPP&CR Regs. 2010]

- The local authority must arrange for each eligible child whom it is looking after to have a personal adviser (PA) [Sch.2 para.19C introduced by s.1 Children (Leaving Care) Act 2000].

- The PA's functions are to:

- Provide advice (including practical advice) and support
- Participate in reviews of her/his case
- Liaise with the responsible authority in the implementation of the pathway plan
- Co-ordinate the provision of services and to take reasonable steps to ensure the child makes use of such services
- Remain informed about the child's progress and wellbeing
- Maintain a written record of contacts with the child [reg.44 CPP& CR Regs.2010]

NB. In R(J) v Caerphilly County Borough Council [2005] EWHC 586(Admin), it was concluded that though not unlawful to appoint as a personal adviser, an employee of the young person's local authority, the assessment and pathway plan must be completed by someone other than the PA whose role is distinct.

R (A) v London Borough of Lambeth [2010] EWHC 1652 makes it clear that the responsible authority cannot avoid its duty in this respect by leaving it to a young person's PA to complete or review a pathway plan.

Relevant & Former Relevant Child: Local Authority Duties

- A *relevant child* [s.23A Children Act 1989 introduced by s.2 Children (Leaving Care) Act 2000 and qualified by virtue of C&YPA 2008 and reg. 3 Care Leavers (England) Regulations 2010] is one aged 16 or 17 who:

  - Is not being looked after by any local authority
  - Is not subject to a Care Order
  - Was, before ceasing to be looked after, an eligible child for purposes described above

- A child is *also* defined as relevant if, as well as satisfying the above criteria, and whilst 16 or over, s/he was (having immediately before admission/detention been looked after for a period/s totalling at least 13 weeks starting after the age of 14):

  - Detained in a remand centre, young offender institution (YOI), secure training centre (STC) or other court-ordered institution, or
  - In a hospital

- In calculating 13 weeks, no account is taken of any period in which child was looked after by a local authority in any of a pre-planned series of short-term placements none of which individually exceeded 4 weeks, at the end of which s/he returned to care of a parent or person with parental responsibility [para.19B (2) Children Act 1989 and reg. 3 Children

(Leaving Care) (England) Regulations 2010 introduced by s.1 Children (Leaving Care) Act 2000].

- Unless arrangement breaks down and s/he ceases to live with that person, a child with a parent/person with parental responsibility/person who had a Residence Order in her/his favour immediately before a Care order was made – for a continuous period of 6 months or more – (whether or not the period began before or after s/he ceased to be looked after) is *not* a 'relevant child' [s.23A (1)-(3) Children Act 1989 and regulation 3(4);(5) Care Leavers (England) Regulations 2010].

- Each local authority must take reasonable steps to keep in touch with a relevant child for whom it is responsible whether s/he is within its area or not [s.23B (1) introduced by s.2 Children (Leaving Care) Act 2000].

- If it has not already appointed one whilst the individual was an eligible child, the local authority must appoint a PA for each relevant child [s.23B (2) introduced by s.2 Children (Leaving Care) Act 2000].

- If a pathway plan has not already been formulated, the local authority must assess need and prepare one [s.23B (3) introduced by s.2 Children (Leaving Care) Act 2000].

  NB. This assessment may be done at the same time as any other one e.g. special needs or disability-related.

Involvement of Relevant or Former Relevant Child [Reg. 4 Care Leavers (England) Regulations 2010]

■ In carrying out an assessment of needs under reg. 5, and in preparing or reviewing a pathway plan under regs. 6 or 7, the responsible authority must, unless it is not reasonably practicable:

  • Seek and have regard to the views of the relevant or former relevant child to whom the assessment or pathway plan relates, and

  • Take all reasonable steps to enable the relevant or former relevant child to attend and participate in any meetings at which their case is to be considered [reg.4(1)]

■ The responsible authority must as soon as practicable provide the relevant or former relevant child with copies of the results of the assessment, the pathway plan and each review of the pathway plan and ensure the contents of each document are explained to the relevant or former relevant child having regard to her/his level of understanding, unless it is not reasonably practicable to do so [reg.4(2)]

■ The responsible authority must ensure that a written record is kept of the views obtained from the young person [reg.4(3)].

Assessment of Needs [Reg.5 Care Leavers (England) Regulations 2010]

■ The responsible authority must assess the needs of each relevant child who does not already have a pathway plan, and each former relevant child falling within s.23CA (*further assistance to pursue education or training*), in accordance with this regulation.

■ The assessment of needs must be completed:

- In the case of a relevant child who does not already have a pathway plan, not more than 3 months after the date on which the child becomes a relevant child, and
- In the case of a former relevant child falling within s.23CA, not more than 3 months after the date on which the responsible authority are informed, in accordance with section 23CA(1)(c), that the former relevant child is pursuing, or wishes to pursue, a programme of education or training [reg.5(1).

■ The responsible authority must ensure that a written record is kept of the:

- Identity of the persons whose views have been sought for the purpose of carrying out the assessment
- Information obtained in the course of the assessment
- Deliberations at any meeting held in connection with any aspect of the assessment, and
- Results of the assessment [reg.5(2)]

■ In carrying out an assessment of the needs of a relevant child who does not already have a pathway plan, the responsible authority must take into account the:

- Child's health and development
- Child's needs for education, training or employment
- Support available to the child from members of the child's family and other persons
- Child's financial needs
- Extent to which the child possesses the practical and other skills necessary for independent living, and
- Child's needs for care, support and accommodation +

■ Unless it is not reasonably practicable or appropriate to do so, the responsible authority must also seek and take into account the views of:

- The child's parents
- Any person who is not the child's parent but has parental responsibility for the child
- Any person who on a day to day basis cares for, or provides accommodation for the child
- Any school or institution within the further education sector attended by the child
- The local authority for the area in which the child lives where that is different from the responsible authority
- The designated teacher at the school where the child is a registered pupil
- Any person providing health care or treatment to the child
- Any person by whom assistance by way of representation is provided to the child by virtue

of arrangements made by the responsible authority under s.26A (*advocacy services*)

- The personal adviser, and
- Any other person whose views the responsible authority, or the child, consider may be relevant [reg.5(3)]

NB. The 'designated teacher' in the case of a maintained school means the member of staff designated by the governing body in accordance with s.20(1) C&YPA 2008. Academies, City Technology Colleges and City Colleges for the Technology of the Arts are required by their Funding Agreements to have a designated teacher. The Designated Teacher (Looked After Pupils etc.)(England) Regulations 2009 (S.I. 2009/1538) made under s.20(3) of the 2008 Act prescribe the qualifications and experience of the designated teacher.

▪ In carrying out an assessment of the needs of a former relevant child falling within s.23CA (*further assistance to pursue education or training*), the responsible authority must take into account:

- The former relevant child's needs for education, training or employment, and
- Any other considerations the responsible authority consider relevant

▪ Unless it is not reasonably practicable to do so, the responsible authority must also seek and take into account the views of:

- The PA, and

- Any other person whose views the responsible authority, or the former relevant child consider may be relevant [reg.5(4)]

Pathway Plans [Reg.6 Care Leavers (England) Regulations 2010]

■ A pathway plan prepared under s.23B(3) (*relevant children*) or s.23CA(3) (*former relevant children*) must be prepared as soon as possible after the assessment of needs referred to in reg. 5 is completed and must include, in particular for a plan prepared for:

- *Relevant children*, the matters referred to in Sch. 1 (reproduced immediately below), and
- *Former relevant children*, the matters referred to in paras. 1 to 4 of Sch.1 [reg.6(1)]

Matters to be Dealt with in the Pathway Plan & Review [Sch. 1 Care Leavers (England) Regulations 2010 in support of Reg.6]

■ The matter are as follows:

- Nature and level of contact and personal support to be provided, and by whom, to the child or young person
- A detailed plan for the education or training of the child or young person
- How the responsible authority will assist the child or young person in relation to employment or other purposeful activity or occupation

- Contingency plans for action to be taken by the responsible authority should the pathway plan for any reason cease to be effective
- Details of the accommodation the child or young person is to occupy (including an assessment of its suitability in the light of the child's or young person's needs, and details of the considerations taken into account in assessing that suitability)
- The support to be provided to enable the child or young person to develop and sustain appropriate family and social relationships
- A programme to develop the practical and other skills necessary for the child or young person to live independently
- The financial support to be provided to the child or young person, in particular where it is to be provided to meet accommodation and maintenance needs
- The health needs, including any mental health needs, of the child or young person, and how they are to be met
- Details of the arrangements made by the authority to meet the child's needs in relation to identity with particular regard to their religious persuasion, racial origin and cultural and linguistic background

- The pathway plan must, in relation to each of the matters included in it set out the:

- Manner in which the responsible authority propose to meet the needs of the relevant or former relevant child, and
- Date by which, and by whom, any action required to implement any aspect of the pathway plan will be carried out [reg.6(2)]

■ The pathway plan must be recorded in writing [reg.6(3)].

Review of Pathway Plans [Reg.7 Care Leavers (England) Regulations 2010]

■ The responsible authority must review the pathway plan of each relevant and former relevant child in accordance with this regulation and arrange a review:

- If requested to do so by the relevant or former relevant child
- If the responsible authority, or the personal adviser, consider a review necessary, and
- In any event, at intervals of not more that 6 months [reg.7(1);(2)]

NB. Relevant authorities are required by s.23E (1D) Children Act to keep pathway plans prepared for relevant children and former relevant children falling within s.23CA under regular review. They are required by s.23C (3)(b) to continue to keep pathway plans of former relevant children under regular review.

■ If the responsible authority provide the relevant child or former relevant child with accommodation under s.23B or s.24B, it must also:

- Arrange a review as soon as is practicable after the end of a period of 28 days beginning on the day on which the accommodation is first provided, and
- On completing such a review determine at what intervals (not exceeding 3 months) subsequent reviews will be carried out [reg.7(3)]

- In carrying out a review the responsible authority must:

  - To the extent it considers it appropriate to do so, seek and take account of the views of the persons mentioned in reg.5(4)(b) or, as the case may be, reg.5(5)(b), (PA and other person the responsible authority or former relevant child consider may be relevant) and
  - Consider whether, in relation to each of the matters set out in the pathway plan, any change is necessary [reg.7(4)]

- The results of the review and any change to the pathway plan must be recorded in writing [reg.7 (5)].

Relevant & Former Relevant Child: Functions of Personal Advisers (PAs) [Reg.8 Care Leavers (England) Regulations 2010]

- A personal adviser has the following functions in relation to the relevant child or former relevant child for whom they are appointed:

  - To provide advice (including practical advice) and support

- When applicable, to participate in the assessment and the preparation of the pathway plan
- To participate in reviews of the pathway plan
- To liaise with the responsible authority in the implementation of the pathway plan
- To co-ordinate the provision of services, and to take reasonable steps to ensure that the child makes use of such services and that they are appropriate to the child's needs
- To remain informed about the relevant child's or former relevant child's progress and wellbeing and
- To keep a written record of contacts with, and of services provided to, the relevant or former relevant child [reg.8(1)]

■ In addition, when accommodation is provided to a relevant child or former relevant child by the responsible authority under s.23B (*assisting a former relevant person aged over 21 who had abandoned education/training set out in her/his pathway plan*) or s.24B (*providing vacation accommodation to a full-time/higher education student*), the PA must visit the relevant child or former relevant child at that accommodation:

- Within 7 days of the accommodation first being provided
- Subsequently, before the pathway plan is reviewed under reg.7(3), and

- At subsequent intervals of not more than 2 months [reg.8(2)]

Support & Accommodation for Relevant Child [Reg.9 & Sch. 2 Care Leavers (England) Regulations 2010]

■ For the purposes of s.23B(8)(c) (*other support for relevant children*), the responsible authority must provide assistance in order to meet the relevant child's needs in relation to education, training or employment as provided for in the pathway plan and or the purposes of s.23B(10), 'suitable accommodation' means accommodation:

- Which so far as reasonably practicable is suitable for the relevant child in the light of her/his needs, including any health needs and any needs arising from any disability
- In respect of which the responsible authority have satisfied itself as to the character and suitability of the landlord or other provider, and
- In respect of which the responsible authority has, so far as reasonably practicable, taken into account the relevant child's wishes and feelings, and education, training or employment needs [reg.9(1)]

■ In determining for the above purposes whether accommodation is suitable for a relevant child, the responsible authority must have regard to the matters set out in Sch.2 with respect to that accommodation i.e:

- Facilities and services provided
- State of repair
- Safety
- Location
- Support
- Tenancy status, and
- Financial commitments involved for the relevant child and their affordability

■ In respect of the relevant child, the matters to be considered are her/his:

- Views about the accommodation,
- Understanding of her/his rights and responsibilities in relation to the accommodation, and
- Understanding of funding arrangements [reg.9(2) & Sch.2]

■ For the purposes of section 24B(5) (*provision of vacation accommodation*):

- 'Higher education' means education provided by means of a course of a description referred to in regulations made under s.22 Teaching and Higher Education Act 1998 and
- 'Further education' has the same meaning as in ss.2(3) and (5) Education Act 1996 except that for the purposes of this regulation it only includes further education which is provided on a full-time residential basis [reg.9(3)]

Records [Reg.10 Care Leavers (England) Regulations 2010]

■ The responsible authority must establish and maintain a written case record for each relevant child and former relevant child ('the case record') which must include the written records required by virtue of reg.4(3) (*views of young person in assessing needs and preparing/reviewing pathway plan*) and reg.5(3) (a) to (c), and the following records ('relevant records'):

- Any assessment of needs
- Any pathway plan
- Any review of a pathway plan [reg.10(1);(2)]

■ Relevant records must be retained by the responsible authority until the 75th anniversary of the date of birth of the relevant or former relevant child to whom they relate or, if the child dies before attaining the age of 18, for a period of 15 years beginning with the date of death [reg.10(3)].

■ The requirement in reg.10(1) may be complied with by retaining the original written records or copies of them, or by keeping all or part of the information contained in them in some other accessible form such as a computer record [reg.10(4)]

■ Relevant records must be kept securely and may not be disclosed to any person except in accordance with:

- Any provision of, or made under or by virtue of, a statute under which access to such records is authorised, or
- Any court order authorising access to such records [reg.10(5)]

Responsible Authority

■ The responsible authority for purposes of a relevant child is the one which last looked after a child [s.23A (4) CA 1989 introduced by s.2 (4) Children (Leaving Care) Act 2000].

Former Relevant Child [s.23C as Introduced by Children (Leaving Care) Act 2000]

■ With respect to a person aged 18 or over, who had been a relevant or eligible child, the local authority which was last the responsible local authority is obliged to:

- Take reasonable steps to keep in touch with the former relevant child whether s/he is in the local authority area or not
- Re-establish contact if it loses touch with her/him
- Continue the appointment of a personal adviser
- Continue to review pathway plan regularly

■ The local authority must also give a former relevant child aged up to 21 years old, to the extent that her/his:

- Welfare requires it, advice and assistance by means of contributing to expenses incurred by living near actual/potential employment
- Welfare and educational or training needs requires it, contributions to expenses incurred by living near the place of actual/potential education/training, or grants for expenses connected with education/training

NB. This support may continue beyond the age of 21 and be transferred to another local authority if the young person moves to a new one (see R v London Borough of Lambeth ex parte Cadell [1998] 1 FLR 253).

■ The local authority must also, to the extent that her/his welfare requires it, give other assistance which may be in kind or in exceptional circumstances cash.

■ The duties described above generally apply until the former relevant child is 21 years old [s.23C (6) introduced by s.2 Children (Leaving Care) Act 2000].

■ If though, the pathway plan sets out a programme of education/training which extends beyond her/his 21st birthday, then the duties associated with that programme continue for as long as the former relevant child pursue that programme [s.23C(7)(a) introduced by s.2 Children (Leaving Care) Act 2000].

NB. Any interruption in pursuance of education/ training programmes must be disregarded if the local authority is satisfied the former relevant child will resume it as soon as reasonably practicable [s.23C(8) introduced by s.2 Children (Leaving Care) Act 2000].

■ A consequent duty if an individual's education/ training programme continues beyond 21, is local authority must keep in touch, maintain a personal adviser and continue to review pathway plan [s.23C (7) (b) introduced by s.2 Children (Leaving Care) Act 2000].

Entitlement to Payment in Respect of Higher Education [s.23C as amended]

■ S.23C Children Act 1989 (*continuing functions of local authorities in respect of 'former relevant children'*) is amended in accordance with s.21(2) –(4) [s.21(1) C&YPA 2008].

■ The result of these amendments is that in addition to providing assistance under s.23C(4), the local authority will have to pay a fixed sum to those who pursue a higher education course.

■ The amount will be determined in regulations (see below), which will also prescribe eligibility criteria, arrangements for making payments (e.g. instalments, intervals between instalments) and circumstances in which instalments may cease or payments be repaid.

■ The duty of the local authority to make payments lasts for as long as the young person follows her/his pathway plan (made under s.23B or s.23CA).

NB. This payment does not affect entitlement to other assistance given under s.23C (4) and will be exempt from tax.

The Children Act 1989 (Higher Education Bursary) (England) Regulations 2009]

■ These regulations are made in exercise of the powers conferred by s.23C (5B) and s.104(4) Children Act 1989.

■ These regulations apply in relation to the payment of the relevant amount for the purposes of s.23C(5A) Children Act 1989 by a local authority in England to a former relevant child who is pursuing a course of higher education started on or after 01.09.08 [reg.1(2)].

■ For the purposes of s.23C(5A) of the Children Act 1989, the relevant amount is currently £2,000 ('the higher education bursary') [reg.2].

■ For the purposes of s.23C(5A) of the Children Act 1989, higher education means a course of higher education that is of at least 2 academic years' duration and is designated by or under regulations made under s.22(1) of the Teaching and Higher Education Act 1998 on the date on which the former relevant child starts the course [reg.3].

■ The local authority may pay the higher education bursary to a former relevant child as a lump sum or by instalments [reg.4 (1)].

■ Before making any decision about payment of the higher education bursary the local authority must, as far as reasonably practicable, ascertain and give due consideration to the wishes and feelings of the former relevant child [reg.4(4)].

■ The local authority may withhold payment of any unpaid balance of the higher education bursary during any period when the former relevant child is not pursuing higher education in accordance with the pathway plan for that person [reg.4(5)].

■ The local authority may recover the whole of the higher education bursary or any part of it from a person to whom payment has been made if there has been a mistake as to the eligibility of that person for the payment [reg.4(6)].

Assistance to Pursue Education or Training [s.23B as amended by s.22(1) C&YPA 2008]

■ S.22(1) amends s.23B Children Act 1989 by omitting subsections 4–7 and inserting after s.23C a new s.23CA thus extending the duty of the local authority so that:

• It must appoint a personal adviser for a 'former relevant child' who informs the responsible local authority (i.e. the one that formerly looked after her/him) that s/he is or intends to pursue a programme of education or training but to whom the local authority would not otherwise have a duty under s.23C because s/he is aged over 21 and has completed or abandoned the programme set out in her/his original pathway plan

- In relation to such an individual aged under 25 (or less if the appropriate national authority prescribe this), the local authority must also carry out an assessment of needs, prepare a pathway plan and provide such assistance as the person's educational and training needs require

NB. The local authority may take into account any payment made under s.23C (5A) when making its assessment of needs.

Extension of Entitlements to Personal Adviser and to Assistance in Connection with Education or Training [s.23]

■ S.23 amends s.23D(1) Children Act 1989 so that the power to make regulations requiring local authorities to appoint personal advisers for certain groups of young people is amended to:

- Extend the upper end of the age range from 21 to 25 years of age
- Extend the upper end of the age range to which the powers for local authorities to provide assistance toward expenses incurred by a young person in education or training apply to age 25

Staying Put (Arrangements for Living with Former Foster Parents After Reaching Adulthood) [s.23CZA introduced by s.98 CFA 2014]

▪ Each local authority in England has the duties described in s.23CZA(3) below in relation to a 'staying put arrangement' i.e. one in which a former relevant child by virtue of s.23C(1)(b) and her/his former foster parent immediately before s/he ceased to be looked after by the local authority, continue to live together after the former relevant child has ceased to be looked after [s.23CZA(2)].

▪ It is the duty of the local authority in discharging the duties in s.23C(3) to monitor the staying put arrangement and to provide advice, assistance and support (this must include financial support) to the former relevant child and former foster parents with a view to maintaining the arrangement until the young person reaches her/his 21st birthday [s.23CZA(3);(4);(6)].

NB. The duty to assist/support etc does not apply if the local authority considers that the staying put arrangements is not consistent with the welfare of the former foster child [s.23CZA(5)].

Retention & Confidentiality of Records [Reg.49–50 Care Planning, Placement & Case Review (England) Regulations 2010]

▪ The responsible authority must establish and maintain a written case record for a child, if one is not already in existence [reg.49(1)].

■ The record must include:

- The child's care plan, including any changes made to that plan and any subsequent plans
- Reports obtained under reg.7 CPP &CR Regs. 2010 (health care)
- Any other document created or considered as part of any assessment of the child's needs or of any review of her/his case
- Any court order relating to the child
- Details of any arrangements have been made by the responsible authority with any other local authority or with an independent fostering agency (IFA) under reg.26 and Sch.5 of CPP & CR Regs. 2010 or with a provider of social work services under which any of the responsible authority's functions in relation to the child are discharged by that local authority or IFA or provider of social work services, details of those arrangements [reg.49(2)]

■ The responsible authority must retain the case record relating to the child either:

- Until the 75th anniversary of her/his birth, or
- If s/he dies before attaining the age of 18, for 15 years beginning with the date of the child's death [reg.50(1) CPP& CR Regs. 2010]

■ The responsible authority must secure the safe keeping of the child's case record and take any necessary steps to ensure that information contained in it is treated as confidential subject only to any:

- Provision of or made under or by virtue of, a statute under which access to such records or information may be obtained or given
- Court order under which access to such records or information may be obtained or given [reg.50(2)]

NB. Failure to keep such records intact and provide access by child to them, may constitute a denial of an individual's right to private and family life under Article 8 of the European Convention seen in Gaskin v UK [1990] 1 FLR 167.

Transfer of Information about Care Leavers [s.24C as amended by Children (Leaving Care) Act 2000]

■ When it appears to a local authority that a person specified in s.24 with whom it has a duty to keep in touch, whom it has been advising or befriending or to whom it has been giving assistance, proposes to live or is living in the area of another local authority, it must inform that authority [s.24C (1) as introduced by Children (Leaving Care) Act 2000].

■ If any one of the following organisations cease to accommodate a child aged 16 or over, it must notify the local authority in whose area s/he proposes to live:

- A voluntary organisation or private children's home after any period of time or
- (Assuming a consecutive period of 3 months or more) any health authority, special health

authority, primary care trust or local education authority, or any care home, independent hospital or any accommodation provided by a NHS trust [s.24C(2) as amended by Children (Leaving Care) Act 2000].

Exclusion from Benefits [s.6 Children (Leaving Care) Act 2000]

- An eligible or relevant child (who by definition is aged less than 18) is not entitled to:

  - Income Based Job-seekers allowance
  - Income Support or
  - Housing Benefit

  NB. S.6 (3) enables the Secretary of State to make regulations to ensure that particular groups are not included e.g. care leavers who are lone parents or disabled.

  There is no provision to remove non-means tested benefits such as Disability Living Allowance which will continue to be paid to any care leavers who qualify for them.

  There is no reference to Council Tax because under 18 year olds are not liable to pay it.

Secure Accommodation for Looked After Children [s.25]

- A looked after child can be placed and kept in secure accommodation only if s/he:

    - Has a history of absconding, and
    - Is likely to abscond from anywhere else, and
    - Is likely, when absconding, to suffer significant harm, or
    - Kept elsewhere, is likely to injure self or others

- The local authority must apply to court for a Secure Accommodation Order and child should be legally represented in accordance with the child's Article 6 rights.

    NB. In Re C [2001] 1 FLR 169 these rights were found not to have been violated even though C's solicitor was only informed of the application for a s.25 order on arrival at court.

- The placement must be reviewed within 28 days of it commencing and thereafter at intervals of no more than 3 months.

- An accommodated child could be placed in security, but parent/s and those with parental responsibility would have a right to remove her/him.

- A child of under 13 cannot be placed in secure accommodation in a children's home without the prior approval of the Secretary of State.

NB. The local authority has discretion to place a child in security for a maximum of 72 hours in 28 days. Children's Guardians will be appointed as per s.41.

▦ The High Court has held that s.25 applications can be considered even where a child is already detained under another statutory power e.g. Mental Health Act 1983.

▦ The wording of the Children Act 1989 and Reg.5 of the Secure Accommodation Regs.1991 should be interpreted to mean it is not necessary for the provisions of s.25 also to be satisfied in the case of a detained child [Hereford & Worcester County Council v S Family Division [1993] 2 FLR 360].

▦ The Court of Appeal has decided neither 'welfare' or 'positive advantage' principles apply, so if the court has found any of s.25 or regulation 6 criteria are satisfied, it must make an Order [Re M (Secure Accommodation Order) [1995] 1 FLR 418].

▦ In Re K (Secure Accommodation Order: Right to Liberty) (Court of Appeal; Dame Elizabeth Butler-Sloss P, Thorpe and Judge LJJ; 15 November 2000), the Court concluded a Secure Accommodation Order is not incompatible with Article 5 of the Convention (Right To Liberty and Security of Person) because it is justified within Article 5(1) (d) as the detention of a minor for the purpose of 'educational supervision'. The latter term should not be equated rigidly with notions of classroom teaching, and particularly in a care context should embrace many aspects of the exercise of parental rights for the benefit and protection of the child concerned.

Remands to Secure Accommodation [s.25 (7)]

■ Subject to specified conditions, a court remanding a male or female aged 12 to 14, or a female aged 15 or 16 to local authority accommodation may, after consultation with the designated authority require that authority to comply with a security requirement i.e. that the child be placed and kept in secure accommodation [s.23 (4) CYPA 1969 as substituted by s.60 CJA 1991 and amended by s.97 (1) CDA 1998].

■ Criteria for imposition of a security requirement are that:

• The individual is charged with or convicted of a violent or sexual offence or an offence punishable in the case of an adult with imprisonment for a term of 14 years more *or*

• S/he is charged with or has been convicted of one or more imprisonable offences which, together with any other imprisonable offences of which s/he has been convicted in any proceedings amount (or would amount if s/he were convicted of the offences with which s/he is charged) to a recent history of repeatedly committing imprisonable offences while remanded on bail or to local authority accommodation *and in addition,*

- The court is of the opinion, after considering all the options for the remand of the individual, that only a secure remand would be adequate either to protect the public from serious harm from her/him *or* to prevent the commission by her/him of imprisonable offences [s.23(5AA) Children and Young Persons' Act 1969 as amended by s.130(3) Criminal Justice and Police Act 2001]

NB. Serious harm is defined in s.161 Powers of Criminal Courts (Sentencing) Act 2000 in relation to sexual and violent offences as 'death or serious personal injury, whether physical or psychological, occasioned by further such offences committed by him'. It is not defined in relation to other offences.

In Re G (Secure Accommodation Order) Family Division; Munby J [2001]1 FLR 884, the court concluded a Youth Court does have jurisdiction to apply the usual criteria of s.25(1) if it is dealing with a child remanded/committed to local authority accommodation.

Complaints & Representations Procedure [ss.26 & 24D as introduced by s.5 Children (Leaving Care) Act 2000]

■ The local authority must establish a procedure for considering any representations (including complaints) made to it about the discharge of any functions under Part III of the Act (i.e. Family Support Services) by:

- Any child looked after or in need
- A child qualifying for advice and assistance
- An eligible or relevant child
- A former relevant child
- Such a child's parent or someone with parental responsibility
- A local authority foster carer
- Such other person as the local authority considers has sufficient interest in the child's welfare,

■ In R v Kingston-upon-Thames Royal Borough ex parte T [1994] 1 FLR 798 it was held that anyone with a grievance should, prior to seeking judicial review, use the s.26 procedures. This was confirmed as the correct approach in R v Birmingham City Council ex parte A [1997] 2 FLR 841.

NB. An applicant in a judicial review must generally show the local authority has acted in a way in which no reasonable authority would have acted (see R v Lancashire CC ex parte M [1992] 1 FLR 109).

Where a complaints panel includes representatives of the local authority, this could be argued to be contrary to Article 6 of the Convention (Right To A Fair Trial Including An Independent and Impartial Tribunal) as in R on the application of Christopher Beeson v Dorset CC and the Secretary of State for Health [200] EWCHA 986 30 November 2001.

s.26 CA 1989 has been amended by s.117 ACA 2002 to extend the scope of complaints and representations procedure to include those functions of Part 4 and 5 of the Children Act 1989 to be specified by the Secretary of State in regulations as well as functions relating to the adoption service offered by the local authority.

Representations & Complaints by Care Leavers [s.117 ACA 2002]

■ The following persons are entitled to make a representation/complaint about 'qualifying functions' (family support services and specified duties in the care/supervision and child protection provisions of the Children Act 1989):

- A child 'qualifying for advice/assistance'
- An 'eligible child'
- A 'relevant child' and
- An individual for whose needs provision is made in the ACA 2002, or such other person the local authority consider has sufficient interest

■ If a local authority receives such a representation/ complaint, it must:

- Provide the local authority officer who has responsibility for such matters with a written summary of that representation/complaint
- Endeavour by informal means to reach a settlement to the satisfaction of the complainant within 14 days and
- If at the end of 14 days no resolution has been reached, notify the local authority officer of that fact [Children Act 1989 Representations Procedure(England) Regulations 2006]

NB. Provisions in Wales are essentially comparable.

Special Guardianship Order Support Services: Representations [14G Children Act 1989]

■ Every local authority is obliged to establish a procedure for considering representations (including complaints) made to it by any person to whom it may provide special guardianship support services about the discharge of its functions under s.14 F (1) in relation to her/him [s.14G(1) Children Act 1989 inserted by ACA 2002].

■ The Children Act 1989 Representations Procedure (England) Regulations 2006 Regulations have been made by the Secretary of State pursuant to s.14G (2) Children Act 1989 (inserted by ACA 2002), providing for such procedures to be in place in relation to any functions associated with the provision of special guardianship support services (see reg. 5)and imposing under reg.9(1) a time limit of 1 year on the making of the above representations, but the regulations go on to provide that a local authority may consider any representations outside the time limit if, having regard to all the circumstances, it concludes that: it would not be reasonable to expect the complainant to have made the representations within the time limit (reg 9(2)(a)) and notwithstanding the time that has passed, it is still possible to consider the representations effectively and fairly

Advocacy Service [s.26A introduced by s.119 ACA 2002]

■ Every local authority must make arrangements for the provision of assistance (including representation) to children or care leavers wishing to use s.26 s.24D respectively to make complaints or representations

■ The Advocacy Services and Representations Procedure (Children) (Amendment) Regulations 2004 SI 719 specify that persons who may *not* provide *such* assistance are those who:

- Are or may be the subject of the representations
- Are responsible for managing the person who is or may be the subject of the representations
- Manage the service which is or may be the subject of the representations

- Have control over the resources allocated to the service which is or may be the subject of the representation

■ Local authorities are obliged to provide a potential or actual complainant with information about advocacy services and offer help in obtaining an advocate.

■ Local authorities must also monitor compliance with the requirements of these regulations.

NB. Provisions in Wales are essentially comparable.

PART IV: CARE & SUPERVISION

Care and Supervision

Duty to Protect Child

- ▨ The proper response to a child thought to be at risk of significant harm is Part IV, *not* s.8 [Nottinghamshire County Council v P [1993] 2 FLR 134].

Attendance of Child at Court

- ▨ Attendance is at court's discretion [s.95].

- ▨ Court may ask for advice from a children's guardian.

   NB. Article 6 of the Convention (Right to a Fair Trial) could be argued to justify child's presence in court.

Applications & Grounds

- ▨ An application may be made only by a local authority or ⚚.S.P.C.C. with respect to a child up to her/his 17th birthday (16th if married) who is suffering or likely to suffer 'significant harm' where the harm, or likelihood of harm, is attributable to the care given, or likely to be given to child, not being what it would be reasonable to expect a parent to give her/him, or child is beyond parental control.

- ▨ The House of Lords has previously determined that the critical date for satisfying the threshold conditions above is the date upon which the local authority initiate protective proceedings [Re M (A

Minor) (Care Order: Threshold Conditions) [1994] 2
FLR 377].

- Re G (Care Proceedings: Threshold Conditions) Re
  [2001] 2 FLR 1111, suggests that evidence gathering
  after the initiation of proceedings and later acquired
  information as to the state of affairs at the time
  proceedings were initiated, could be taken into
  account by a court.

- In Re C and B (Care Order: Future Harm) [2001] 1
  FLR 611, the Court of Appeal emphasised the
  principle of proportionality in Article 8 of the
  European Convention required that action taken by a
  local authority must be a proportionate response to
  the feared harm.

- In the above case, 2 older children of the family had
  been made subject of Care Orders in 1996. After a
  report from an independent social worker assessing
  that these facts disclosed a risk to the 3rd child then
  aged 10 months and doing well in the care of its
  mother, the local authority applied for an Emergency
  Protection Order on the 4th child on the day of its
  birth and an interim order on the 3rd child. The Court
  of Appeal found that the local authority had not
  taken the time to explore alternative options and that
  its actions were not proportionate.

- The House of Lords has ruled that in interpreting the
  phrase 'the care given to the child', that phrase refers
  primarily to the care given by parent/s or other
  primary carers, but where care is shared, the phrase

can embrace the care given by *any* of the carers. This interpretation was necessary to allow the Court to intervene to protect a child who was clearly at risk, even though it was not possible to identify the source of the risk [Lancashire CC v B [2000] 1 FLR 583].In addition, it has been decided by the House of Lords in Re O and ☖ and Re B[[2003] 1 FLR 1169] that where it was impossible to tell which of 2 parents had inflicted the injuries or whether both had done so, then the threshold criteria were met.

NB. Where a child suffered significant harm but the court was unable to identify which parent had been the perpetrator, or indeed, whether both had been, the court should proceed at the welfare stage on the footing that each parent was a possible perpetrator i.e. it would be wrong, if, because neither parent had been proved to be the perpetrator, the court had to proceed at the welfare stage as though child was not at risk from either parent even though one or other of them was the perpetrator of significant harm [Re O and ☖; Re B [2–3] 1 FLR 1169 HL]

Definition of 'Harm'

- 'Harm' is defined as: ill treatment (including sexual and non-physical abuse) or impairment of health (physical or mental) or development (physical, intellectual, emotional, social or behavioural), including for example impairment suffered from seeing or hearing the ill-treatment of another [s.31 as amended by s.120 ACA 2002].

■ 'Significant' in relation to health or development is: In comparison to what could reasonably be expected of a similar child.

■ In Re O (A Minor) (Care Order: Education Procedure) [1992] 2 FLR 7 it was found that the relevant comparison was with a child of similar intellectual and social development who has gone to school, not with an average child who may or may not have attended properly.

■ In a case heard by the House of Lords, Re H and R (Child Sexual Abuse: Standards of Proof) [1996] 1 FLR 80, L.R., it was determined that:

- In s.31(2) 'likelihood of harm' is established if, court concludes is a real or substantial risk of significant harm in future (harm does not have to be shown as being more probable than not)
- The required standard of proof for an allegation of sexual abuse is balance of probabilities, taking account of the fact that the more improbable the event, the stronger must be the evidence that it *did* occur, before on the balance of probability, its occurrence would be established

NB. This approach has been confirmed as being the correct one in the Court of Appeal decisions in Re U and Re B [2004] 2 FLR 263, which followed on the case of Angela Cannings, and rejected the suggestion made by Bodey J in Re ET [2003] 2FLR 1205 that the difference between the civil and criminal standards of proof was largely illusory.

- In order to rely upon past events to establish the threshold criteria these facts must be proved to the required standard

▪ More recently in B (Children) [2008] UKHL 35, it was made clear there was only *one* civil standard of proof i.e. that the fact in question more probably occurred than not. Neither the seriousness of an allegation or its consequences should make any difference to the standard of proof in determining a fact. Common sense, not law required that in deciding whether it was more likely than not something had taken place, regard should be had to inherent probabilities. If a judge found it more likely than not an event took place, then it was to be treated as having done so and vice versa.

NB. In the Matter of J (Children) [2013] UKSC 9 the Supreme Court rejected an appeal by local authority which had contended that a child could be regarded as 'likely to suffer' harm for the purposes of s 31(2) of the Children Act 1989 if another child has been harmed in the past and there was a possibility that the parent now caring for her/him was responsible for the harm to the other child.

Care Plans [s.31 (3A)]

▪ No Care Order may be made until the court has considered a 's.31A plan' (court care plan).

▪ Where a full Care Order might be made, the appropriate local authority (the one to be designated in any order) and all parties must, within a time-scale directed by the court follow the arrangements laid down in the Public Law Outline (PLO) as revised in 2014.

■ While the application is pending, the authority must keep its s.31A plan under review and revise it as the authority consider necessary.

NB. With respect to an apparent 'shaken baby syndrome case', Mrs Justice Theis's judgment in the case of London Borough of Islington v Al Alas and Wray [2012] EWHC 865 (Fam) should be explored.

Twin-Track Planning

■ In Re D and Another (Children) (Care Plan: Twin Track Planning) [1999] 4 All ER, Bracewell J. stated that in order to prevent delays in providing permanency, it is incumbent on local authorities and children's guardians to identify clearly the options available for the court by 'twin track' planning, rather than the conventional sequential approach.

■ The 'Handbook of Best Practice in Children Act Cases' published by the then Children Act Advisory Committee in 1997 stated.' if the plan is for an adoptive placement, the court will be handicapped in assessing the plan and times-scale unless the child concerned has already been considered and approved by the adoption and fostering panel and potential suitable adoptive families have been identified. It is not good practice to await the making of a Care Order before obtaining such information'.

Human Rights

■ In Home Office Human Rights Act 1998 'Core Guidance' it is suggested the principle of 'proportionality' used by the European Court requires that if action is taken breaching the right to family life under Article 8(1) which is then justified by reference to Article 8(2), such action must be proportionate to the end set out in Article 8(2).

■ The Core Guidance paraphrases this as 'not taking a sledgehammer to crack a nut' and the example given of proportionality is that of Care Proceedings.

■ In Re O (Supervision Order) [2001] 1 FLR 923, in the Court of Appeal, the importance of 'proportionality' of intervention was reinforced where an appeal by a local authority against a refusal to make a Care Order was dismissed and a Supervision Order confirmed as adequate for the particular circumstances.

NB. An allegation made in Care Proceedings that a local authority has breached the ECHR should be dealt with in those care proceedings (Re V [2004])1 FLR 944).

NB. In T (Children) [2012] UKSC 36 the Supreme Court has made clear that it is inappropriate to expect a local authority to make good any deficiency in the provision of legal aid, in relation to a party to proceedings brought by a local authority to safeguard the welfare of children. This decision establishes that where allegations are made by a local authority in such proceedings, which are not ultimately proven, and it was reasonable that those allegations be investigated by a court, justice does not demand that the local authority should be responsible for the legal costs of a person against whom the allegations are made who did not have the benefit of public funding

Timetabling of Care, Supervision & Other Family Proceedings [s.32 as amended by s.14 CFA 2014]

- ■ A court hearing an application for an order under part IV (care and supervision) must draw up a timetable for disposing of the application:

  - Without delay and
  - In any event, within 26 weeks beginning with the day on which the application as issued [s.32(1)]

- ■ A court when drawing up a timetable must in particular have regard to the impact which the timetable would have on the:

  - Welfare of the child to whom the application relates and
  - Conduct of the proceedings [s.32(3)]

NB. The above issues also have to be applied to revising the timetable or extending it. The expectation is completion within 26 weeks unless specifically justified.

■ If a court consider that an extension *is* necessary to enable the court to resolve the proceedings justly [s.32(5)] each separate extension (and there can be more than one) should last no more than 8 weeks. Guidance notes accompanying the CFA 2014 suggest that reasons for extensions might relate to parallel criminal proceedings or a disability/other impairment of a person involved in the proceedings.

NB. The President of the Family Division has noted in (Re B-S (Children) (Adoption Order: Leave to Oppose) [2013] EWCA Civ 1146 that 'the 26 weeks rule is not, and must never be allowed to become, a straightjacket, least of all if rigorous adherence to an inflexible timetable risks putting justice in jeopardy', and my endorsement (para 29) of Pauffley J's warning in Re NL (A child) (Appeal: Interim Care Order: Facts and Reasons) [2014] EWHC 270 (Fam), [2014] 1 FLR 1384, that 'Justice must never be sacrificed upon the altar of speed.'

NB. In Re W (Children) [2014] EWFC 22 the President of the Family Division has also affirmed that the court expects and will now demand strict compliance with court orders.

Effects/ Duration of Care Order [ss.33; 34 as amended by Sch.3 paras. 63; 64 ACA 2002]

■ A Care Order:

• Gives the local authority parental responsibility and the right to decide to what extent parent,

> guardian, special guardian or a person who has parental responsibility by virtue of s.4A can meet their continuing parental responsibility
- Lasts until child is 18

NB. This may be argued to be in breach of the child's right to family life under Article 8(1)

- Discharges any existing Supervision Order (S.O.), Education Supervision (E.S.O), s.8, School Attendance Order and, if child a Ward of Court, that Wardship
- Assumes contact with parent/s, guardian or special guardian, previous holders of Residence Orders, anyone who has parental responsibility by virtue of s.4A or persons with care of child by virtue of Order under High Court's inherent jurisdiction and the local authority 'contact plan' will be considered before a Care Order is made

- ■ On an application by those cited immediately above or others (with leave of court), the court may direct contact arrangements [see also Local Authority Duties towards Looked After Children p. 88].

Control of Expert Evidence & Assessments in Children's Proceedings [s.13 CFA 2014]

- ■ A person may *not* without the permission of the court instruct a person to provide expert evidence for use in children's proceedings and if this is done the evidence derived is inadmissible (unless the court rules otherwise) [s.13(1);(2) CFA 2014].

- A person may not without permission of the court cause a child to be medically or psychiatrically examined or otherwise assessed for the purpose of the provision of expert evidence in children's proceedings and if this is done resulting evidence is inadmissible (unless the court rules otherwise) [s.13(3);(4) CFA 2014].

- In children's proceedings a person may not without permission of the court put expert evidence (in any form) before the court and the court may give permission in this and the above situations only if it is of the opinion that the expert evidence is necessary to assist the court to resolve the proceedings justly [s.13(5);(6) CFA 2014].

- When deciding whether to give permission in any of the above situations, the court is to have regard in particular to:

  - Any impact which giving permission would be likely to have on the welfare of the children concerned, including the impact of a medical/psychiatric examination would be likely to have
  - The issues to which the expert evidence would relate
  - The questions which the court would require the expert to answer
  - What other expert evidence is available (obtained before or after the start of proceedings)
  - Whether evidence could be given by another person on the matters which the expert would give evidence

- The impact which giving permission would be likely to have on the timetable for, and duration and conduct of the proceedings
- The cost of the expert evidence and
- Any matters prescribed by Family Procedure Rules [s.13(7) CFA 2014]

NB. Conditions about acceptance of 'expert evidence' do not apply to local authority staff nor Cafcass/ Cafcass Cymru.

Court's Decision to Grant a Care Order [s.31 as amended by s.15 CFA 2014]

■ A court deciding whether to make a Care Order:

- Is required to consider the permanence provisions of the s.31A plan for the child concerned but
- Is *not* required to consider the remainder of the plan (subject to s.34(11) – contact arrangements) [s.31(3A) substituted by s.15 CFA 2014]

NB. The fact that the court does not have to address the remainder of the plan does not prevent it from doing so.

■ The permanence provisions set out the long-term plan for the upbringing of the child and provide for any of the following:

- The child to live with any parent of the child or with any other member of, or any friend of her/ his family
- Adoption

- Long-term care in neither of the above settings [s.31(3B)]

NB. S.16 CFA 2014 introduces the possibility that regulations may be made about permanence provisions and time limits for disposals.

■ In Re DE (A Child) [2014] EWFC 6 Baker J has set out guidance, approved by the President of the Family Division, in relation to cases where a child remains at home under a Care Order.

Limiting/Refusing Contact for Child in Care [s.34 as amended by s.8 CFA 2014]

Contact Plan

- Subject to the provisions of s.34 and s.22 (3) (a) CA 1989 (duty to safeguard and promote welfare) a local authority must allow the child reasonable contact with parents, any guardian and any person named in a Child Arrangements Order as a person with whom the child was to live immediately before the Care Order was made [s.34 (1) as amended].

  NB. If allowing contact with any of those persons would not safeguard and promote the welfare of the child, the local authority should not allow it. S.34 (4) allows the Secretary of State to issue regulations detailing matters a local authority should be considering.

- Courts must, before making, varying or discharging an Order under s.34, consider and invite parties to comment on proposed contact arrangements between child and parents and other involved relatives [s.34 (11) as amended].

  NB. Routine acceptance by courts of the local authority's proposals or of 'contact at the discretion of the local authority' could be argued to be breach of Article 8 of the Convention.

■ Directions as to contact may be given on the court's initiative or as a response to an application made by :

- The local authority
- The child
- Parent/guardian/special guardian/person with parental responsibility by virtue of s.4A
- A person named in a Child Arrangements Order as person with whom the child was to live, or had care of the child by virtue of an order made under the High Court's inherent jurisdiction, immediately before the Care Order was made
- Any other person who has obtained the court's permission

NB. Contact may be by means of letters, e-mails, text messages, telephone, photographs or any other method as well as visits. Local authorities are empowered to help with the cost of visiting looked after children where there would otherwise be undue hardship [Sch.2 para.1].

Planned Refusal of Contact [s.34 (4)]

■ In response to an application by the local authority or child, the court may make an order which allows the local authority to refuse contact between the child and any of the persons listed in the contact plan section above.

■ Orders under s.34 can be made at the same time the Care Order is made or later, and may be varied or discharged on the application of the local authority, child or the person named in the order.

■ When a local authority is authorised under s.34 to refuse contact with a parent/s, other person who holds parental responsibility, relative, friend or connected person, the duty to endeavour to promote contact between the child and that person does *not* apply [s.6A inserted by s.8(3) CFA 2014].

NB. What a local authority in England must have regard to in considering contact between a child and any person listed in s.34(1) is whether it would be consistent with safeguarding and promoting the child's welfare [s.34(8)(za) CA 1989].

Emergency Refusal of Contact [s.34 (6) & Reg.8 CPP&CR (England) Regs.2010]

■ Reg. 8 applies if a child is in the care of the responsible authority and the responsible authority has decided under s.34 (6) CA 1989 (*refusal of contact as a matter of urgency*) to refuse to allow contact that would otherwise be required by virtue of s.34 (1) or an order under s.34 (*parental contact etc with a child in care*) [reg.8 (1)].

■ The responsible authority must immediately send written notification to the following persons of the information specified in reg.8(3) below:

- The child, unless it would not be appropriate to do so having regard to her/his age and understanding

- The parent, other person with parental responsibility or (if the child was in the care of the responsible authority for the child immediately before the Care Order was made), a person named in a Child Arrangements Order as a person with whom the child was to live was made
- If, immediately before the Care Order was made a person had care of the child by virtue of an order made in exercise of the High Court's inherent jurisdiction with respect to children, that person
- Any other person whose wishes and feelings the responsible authority consider to be relevant, and
- The IRO [reg.8(2) CPP& CR 2010]

■ The information specified in reg.8(2) above is:

- The responsible authority's decision
- Date of the decision
- Reasons for the decision
- Duration of the decision (if applicable), and
- Remedies available in case of dissatisfaction [reg.8(3) CPP& CR 2010]

■ The responsible authority may depart from the terms of any order made under s.34 CA 1989 by agreement with the person in relation to whom the order is made, provided that:

- The child, being of sufficient understanding, also agrees, and

- Written notification of the specified information is sent within 5 working days to the persons specified in reg.8(2) [reg.8(4) CPP& CR 2010]

■ If the responsibly authority has decided to vary or suspend any arrangement made (otherwise than under an order under s.34) with a view to affording any person contact with the child, it must immediately give written notification containing the specified information to the persons listed in reg.8(2) [reg.8(5) CPP& CR 2010].

■ The responsible authority must record any decision made under this regulation in the child's care plan [reg.8(6) CPP& CR 2010].

NB. Where the court concurs with the local authority view there should be no contact with a child, it should make no order for contact because such an action would confer no advantage on the local authority [Kent CC v. C 1993 Fam. 557].

■ When, by virtue of emergency refusal of contact under s.34(6) a local authority is entitled to refuse to allow contact between the child and any of those specified in Sch.2 para. 15(1) (a)-(c), it is not obliged to try to promote contact between the child and that person [s.34(6A) inserted by s.8 CFA 2014]

■ In Re T (Termination of Contact: Discharge of Order [1997] 1 FLR 517 CA), the Court of Appeal considered in what circumstances a court should discharge an order made under s.34(4) authorising a local authority to refuse contact to a child in care and determined that:

- On an application to discharge, the court should not re-investigate propriety of the original order
- Applicant must .'as a threshold test , show circumstances have changed sufficiently to make application a genuine one'
- Once that test is satisfied, court should determine the application pursuant to s.1 Children Act 1989
- If, on the facts at the Hearing of such an application a s.34(4) order would not be justified then it should be discharged

■ The court also suggested making such an order would not be right unless there is no realistic possibility of the child's rehabilitation with person in question, a probable need to terminate contact is foreseeable and is not too remote.

NB. Failure to consider the position of all those who might potentially have a contact relationship with a child e.g. an uncle, has successfully been argued to breach both uncle and child's rights under Article 8(1) of the Convention in Boyle v UK [1994] 19 EHRR 179.

Effects/ Duration of Supervision Order [s.35; Sch.3 parts 1 & 2]

■ A Supervision Order (SO):

- Requires supervisor to advise, assist and befriend

- Lasts 12 months, can be varied by court to a Care Order, discharged, or renewed to max of 3 years
- Imposes obligations on a 'responsible person' (i.e. person with parental responsibility or with whom child living) to take reasonable steps to ensure compliance of child with Supervision Order and that s/he also complies with directions given

NB. The High Court has ruled that the construction of paras 2 & 3 of Sch.3 permits a court to direct that a 'responsible person' live with a child in a particular place [Croydon London Borough Council v A (No. 3) Family Division 03.07.92]. However the Act suggests that it is the Supervisor, not the court, who has authority to direct. This determination, begs the question of the responsible person's refusal to consent.

The Court of Appeal ruled in T v Wakefield Metropolitan District Council [2008] EWCA Civ 199 that Sch.3 para.6 did not permit the making of a SO of 3 years' duration from the outset.

Exclusion Requirements in Interim Care Orders [s.38A (3) as inserted by s.52 & Sch.6 FLA 1996]

- Provisions described below enable the court when making an Interim Care Order, to attach an exclusion requirement so a suspected abuser can be removed/ kept away from the home in which the child is living or from the surrounding area.

- If the court is satisfied that there are reasonable grounds for believing the threshold criteria for Care and Supervision (s.31) are met, and consequently makes an I.C.O., the court may include an 'exclusion requirement' *if*:

  - It is reasonable cause to believe if a 'relevant person' is excluded from a dwelling-house in which child lives, s/he will cease to suffer/be likely to suffer significant harm and
  - Another person living in the same dwelling-house (parent or other person) is able/willing to give the child the care which it would be reasonable to expect a parent to give, and consents to it [s.38A as inserted by s.52 Sch.6 FLA 1996]

- An 'exclusion requirement' is any 1 or more of the following provisions which may:

  - Require the relevant person to leave a dwelling-house in which s/he is living with the child
  - Prohibit the relevant person from entering a dwelling-house in which the child lives, e.g. if the local authority places the child with a relative
  - Exclude the relevant person from a defined area in which a dwelling-house is included and in which the child is situated, e.g. if the local authority places her/him with a relative

Duration of Exclusion Requirements in Interim Care Orders [s.38A (4) as inserted by s.52 & Sch.6 FLA 1996]

■ Court may provide that the exclusion requirement is to have effect for a shorter period than other provisions of an Interim Care Order.

NB. There is no power to extend exclusion requirements beyond interim or Emergency Protection Order stage. If continuing protection is sought, application must be made by person with whom child living for an injunction under s.100 or a Prohibited Steps Order.

Power of Arrest [s.38A (5) as inserted by s.52 & Sch.6 FLA 1996]

■ Exclusion requirements may have a power of arrest attached [s.38A (5) as inserted by s.52 and Sch.6 FLA 1996].

■ Where a power of arrest is attached, a court may provide it is to have effect for a shorter period than exclusion requirement.

NB. Any period specified for purpose of ss.4 or 6 above, may be extended by court on 1 or more occasion on application to vary or discharge an Interim Care Order [s.38A (7) CA 1989 inserted by s.52 and Sch.6 FLA 1996].

■ Where a power of arrest is attached to an exclusion requirement of an Interim Care Order, a constable may arrest without warrant, any person whom s/he has reasonable cause to believe is in breach of requirement [s.38A (8) as inserted by s.52 and Sch.6 FLA 1996].

- If, while an Interim Care Order with exclusion requirements is in force, local authority has removed a child from dwelling-house from which 'relevant person' is excluded to other accommodation for a continuous period of over 24 hours, the exclusion requirement ceases [s.38A (10) as inserted by s.52 and Sch.6 FLA 1996].

Undertakings Relating to Interim Care Orders [s.38B as inserted by s.52 Sch.6 FLA 1996]

- In any case where court has power to include an exclusion requirement in Interim Care Order, it may accept an undertaking from a relevant person.

- In such cases no power of arrest may be attached [s.38B (1) & (2) as inserted by s.52 & Sch.6 FLA 1996].

- Such an undertaking will:

  - Be enforceable as if it were an order of the court
  - Cease to have effect if, whilst in force, local authority removes child from dwelling-house from which relevant person excluded, to other accommodation for a continuous period of over 24 hours [s.38B(3) CA 1989 as inserted by s.52 & Sch.6 FLA 1996]

■ On the application of a person not entitled to apply for discharge/variation of Care Order/Supervision Order, but who is a person to whom an exclusion requirement contained in the order applies, an Interim Care Order may be varied/discharged by the court in so far as it imposes the exclusion requirement [s.39 (3A) as inserted by s.52 & Sch. 6 FLA 1996].

■ If a power of arrest has been attached to an exclusion requirement of an Interim Care Order, the court may, on the application of any person entitled to apply for the discharge of the order so far as it imposes the exclusion requirement, vary or discharge the order in so far as it confers a power of arrest (regardless of whether any application has been made to vary/ discharge any other provision) [s.39(3B) CA 1989 as inserted by s.52 & Sch.6 FLA 1996].

Best Practice in Care Proceedings

■ In Re E and Others (Minors) (Care Proceedings: Social Work Practice) [2000] 2 FLR 254 FD, Bracewell J issued the following guidelines:

• The top document of every social work file should be a running chronology of significant events kept up to date to facilitate identification of serious and deep rooted problems rather than the circumstances triggering the instant referral

• Lack of parental co-operation was never a reason to close a file or remove a child from a protection register (it was instead justification for more intense investigation)

- Referrals from professionals should be given great weight and investigated thoroughly
- Line managers and others with decision making power should never make a judgement to take no action without full knowledge of file and consulting those professionals who knew family
- Siblings should not be considered in isolation, but in context of family history taking account of problems and results of intervention with respect to previous children
- To avoid drift, work with families has to be time limited and require changes within time scales

Education Supervision Orders (E.S.O.) [s.36]

Applications

- By the Local Education authority (LEA) following consultation with Children's Social Care.

Grounds

- Court must be satisfied child of compulsory school age and not being properly educated (i.e. receiving efficient full-time education suitable to her/his age, ability, aptitude and any special educational needs).

  NB. An Education Supervision Order may not be made for a child in care, but is possible for one who is accommodated.

Effect [Sch.3 para.12]

■ Child under supervision of the LEA and the supervisor must:

- Advise, assist, befriend and give directions to child/parents to secure proper education
- Consider, where directions given have not been complied with, what further steps to take

NB. Before giving directions, the supervisor must, so far as is reasonably practicable, ascertain wishes/ feelings of child/parents, in particular desired place of education.

Duration [Sch.3 para.15]

■ Initially 1 year but may be extended on more than 1 occasion for up to 3 years at a time.

■ Ceases if child attains school leaving age or is made subject of a Care Order.

Discharge & Variation of Care Order, Supervision Order & Education Supervision Order [ss.39; 91; Sch.3 para.17]

■ Care Order by person with parental responsibility, child or local authority.

■ Supervision Order by person with parental responsibility, child or supervisor.

■ Education Supervision Order by child, parent or local education authority.

NB. If an application has been made for discharge of a Care Order, Supervision Order, no further application may be made within 6 months without the leave of the court.

Children's Guardians

■ Children's guardians are employed or engaged by the Children and Family Courts Advisory and Support Service (Cafcass).

■ They play an active role as representatives for the child and advisors to the court on e.g. time-tabling and directions.

Function	Title
Report by CAFCASS officer s.7(1) (a)	Children and Family Reporter
Report by local authority s.7(1) (b)	Welfare Officer
Representation of child in public law proceedings s.41	Children's Guardian
Representation of child subject in adoption case	Children's Guardian
Parental consent in adoption	Reporting Officer
Representation of child in Human Fertilisation and Embryology Act 1990 case	Parental Order Reporter

■ For 'specified proceedings' (Care, Supervision, Child Assessment, Emergency Protection Orders, making or revocation of Placement Orders and making , varying or discharging s.8 orders) the court must appoint a children's guardian unless satisfied this is unnecessary [s.41 as amended by s.122 ACA 2002].

▪ Children's guardians have a right of access to all records concerning the child belonging to or held by the local authority or the N.S.P.C.C. [s.42 (1)].

NB. The role of a children's guardian comes to an end with the proceedings in respect of which s/he has been appointed [Re M Prohibited Steps Order: Application for Leave FD 24.08.92].

A local authority cannot interfere with the manner in which children's guardians carry out their duties (following an attempt to impose a maximum number of hours for various reports) [R v Cornwall County Council ex parte G [1992] 1 PLR 270].

Investigation by Local Authority of Need for Care or Supervision Order [s.37]

▪ In any family proceedings, if the court feels a Care or Supervision Order may be necessary it can ask the local authority to investigate.

▪ A report of the local authority's findings should normally be provided to the court within 8 weeks [s.37 (4)].

Jurisdiction of High Court

■ In the matter of A (Children) [2013] UKSC 60, the Supreme Court unanimously decided that the High Court of England and Wales has jurisdiction to order the 'return' to this country of a small child even though he has never been present here.

PARTS VI–XII: PRIVATE FOSTERING & MISCELLANEOUS

Private Fostering [Part X]

Definition [s.66]

■ Child under 16 (18 if disabled) and cared for and accommodated by non-relative, or someone without parental responsibility for over 27 days.

Requirements [Sch.8 and relevant regulations]

■ Foster carer must notify local authority.

■ Local authority has a duty to inspect [s.67].

NB. Unless siblings or local authority grants exemption, there is a 'usual fostering limit' of 3 children (i.e. 4 or more becomes a Children's Home).

Voluntary and Private Homes [Part VII & VIII]

■ Voluntary and private homes have similar duties to local authorities [ss.61&64].

■ The Office for Standards in Education (Ofsted) and the National Assembly (in Wales) are accountable for inspection (Care Standards Act 2000).

Miscellaneous

Notification to Relevant Local Authority about Children Placed by Health/ Education Bodies [s.85 as amended]

■ If the above organisations do, or plan to, accommodate a child for 3 months or more, they must notify the Director of Children's Service (in Wales the Director of Children and Young People's Services) in the relevant local authority.

NB. Notifications must be to the 'appropriate officer' (the Director of Children's Services in England where the child is ordinarily resident (Lead Director for Children & Young Persons for a local authority in Wales) [s.17 C&YPA 2008]

Notification to Relevant Local Authority about Children Accommodated by Care Homes & Independent Hospitals [ss.85; 86 as amended]

■ If the above organisations do, or plan to, accommodate a child for 3 months or more, they must notify the Director of Children's Service (in Wales the Director of Children and Young People's Services) in the relevant local authority.

NB. In this case the relevant authority is the one in which the establishment is located.

Notification to Relevant Local Authority about Children Accommodated by Care Homes & Independent Hospitals [ss.85; 86 as amended]

■ The local authority notified under s.85 or s.86 must take reasonable steps to determine if child's welfare is adequately safeguarded and promoted [s.86].

■ S.18 C&YPA 2008 inserted a new s.86A into the Children Act 1989 (*visitors for children notified to the local authority under ss.85 or 86*) and applies if the appropriate officer of a local authority:

  • Has been notified with respect to a child under s. 85(1) (accommodated by health bodies or local education authorities) or s.86(1) (care home or independent hospital) and
  • Has not been notified with respect to that child under s.85(2) or, as the case may be, s.86(2) i.e. that the child has ceased to be so accommodated [s.86A Children Act 1989 as inserted by s.18 C&YPA 2008]

■ The local authority must, in accordance with regulations made under s.86A (see below), make arrangements for the child to be visited by a 'representative' of the authority [s.86A(2)].

■ It is the function of a representative to provide advice and assistance to the local authority on the performance of its duties under s.85(4) or s.86(3) (i.e. to take such steps as are reasonably practicable to enable it to determine whether the child's welfare is adequately safeguarded and promoted and consider the extent to which (if at all) it should exercise any of its functions under the Children Act 1989) [s.86A(3)].

NB. The local authority might conclude that the child is 'in need' as per s.17 Children Act 1989 and requires family support services.

▪ Those regulations under s.86A Children Act 1989 (Accommodated Children Visiting Arrangement Regulations (England) 2010) make provision about:

- The frequency of visits under visiting arrangements
- Circumstances in which visiting arrangements must require a child to be visited; and
- Additional functions of a representative [s.86A(4) inserted by s.18 C&YPA 2008]

▪ Regulations under s.86 are to be made by the Secretary of State and the Welsh Ministers acting jointly [s.86A (5)].

▪ In choosing its representative a local authority must satisfy themselves that the person chosen has the necessary skills and experience to perform the functions of a representative [s.86A(6)].

Independent Schools [s.87 (1)-(5) as amended by s.105 Care Standards Act 2000]

▪ When such schools accommodate children, they must safeguard and promote their welfare.

- Ofsted (or in Wales the National Assembly) has a duty to check this and a right to enter premises at any reasonable time.

Admissibility of Child's Evidence [s.96]

- If court believes child does not understand nature of oath her/his evidence may still be heard if, in court's opinion:

  - Child does understand s/he has a duty to tell the truth, and
  - S/he has sufficient understanding to justify evidence being heard

  NB. Re W (Children) [2010] UKSC 12 [2010] 2 FLR dealt with the principles to be applied in the exercise of the court's discretion in deciding whether a child should attend and give evidence in family proceedings. The essential test is whether justice can be done to all parties without further questioning of the child. The Supreme Court predicted that the consequence of the balancing exercise would usually be that the benefits of calling the child would not outweigh the additional harm to be done to her/him but that rarity should be a consequence of the exercise, rather than a threshold test.

- The child's statement or a statement by another person concerning the upbringing, maintenance or welfare of the child is admissible (notwithstanding the normal hearsay rule).

■ Hearsay evidence is admissible in all Children Act
   proceedings in a magistrates' court including an
   application for a Secure Accommodation Order [R.(J.)
   v. Oxfordshire County Council [1992] All ER 660]
   and presumably an application for an E.P.O.

Self-Incrimination [s.98]

■ In any proceedings in which a court is hearing an
   application for an order under Part IV or V of the
   Children Act 1989, no person is excused (on the
   grounds that doing so might incriminate her/him or
   spouse) from:

   • Giving evidence on any matter
   • Answering any question put in the course of
      giving evidence

■ A statement or admission made in such proceedings
   shall not be admissible in evidence against the
   person making it or spouse in proceedings for an
   offence other than perjury.

   *NB. See Re C [1996] 2 FLR 725 and Re M (Care
   Proceedings: Disclosure) [2001] 2 FLR 1316*

Police Investigation: Privilege

■ The House of Lords affirmed in Re L (Police
   Investigation: Privilege) [1996] 1 FLR 731 HL, that:

   • In proceedings under the Act the better view is
      that no privilege attaches to expert reports or

indeed to anything except direct solicitor/client communications and

- Accordingly, the present practice of requiring disclosure as a condition of obtaining leave for expert evidence is proper.

NB. The above decision of the House of Lords is reinforced by Article 6 (Right to a Fair Trial) which encompasses the notion of full disclosure to all parties of all relevant documents.

B

CHILD PROTECTION

Principles of Effective Safeguarding

■ Effective safeguarding arrangements in every local authority should be underpinned by two key principles:

- Safeguarding is everybody's responsibility: each professional and organisation should play their full part
- Child-centred approach: services should be based upon a clear understanding of the needs and views of children

Safeguarding is Everyone's Responsibility

■ Everyone who works with children – including teachers, GPs, nurses, midwives, health visitors, early years professionals, youth workers, police officers, A&E staff, paediatricians, voluntary and community workers and social workers has a responsibility for keeping them safe.

■ Local arrangements need to be strongly led and promoted at a local level, specifically by:

- A strong lead from local authority members, and the commitment of chief officers in all agencies, in particular the Director of Children's Services (DCS) and Lead Member (LM) for Children's Services in each local authority and
- Effective local coordination and challenge by the LSCBs in each area

A Child-centred Approach

■ Anyone working with children should see and speak to the child; listen to what they say; take their views seriously; and work with them collaboratively when deciding how to support their needs.

■ Everyone who works with children – including teachers, GPs, nurses, midwives, health visitors, early years professionals, youth workers, police officers, A&E staff, paediatricians, voluntary and community workers and social workers has a responsibility for keeping them safe.

- A child-centred approach is supported by the:
- Children Act 1989 (as amended by s.53 Children Act 2004) which requires local authorities to give due regard to a child's wishes when determining what services to provide under s.17 and before making decisions about action to be taken to protect individual children under s.47 Children Act 1989 (these duties are in addition to the duties about establishing wishes and feelings of children who are, or may be, looked after (s.22 (4) including those who are provided with accommodation under s.20 and children taken into police protection (s.46(3) (d)
- Equality Act 2010 which puts a responsibility on public authorities to have due regard to the need to eliminate discrimination and promote equality of opportunity; this applies to the process of identification of need and risk faced by the individual child and the process of assessment;

no child or group of children must be treated any less favourably than others in being able to access effective services which meet their particular needs

- United Nations Convention on the Rights of the Child (UNCRC), an international agreement that protects the rights of children and provides a child-centred framework for the development of services to children; the UK Government ratified the UNCRC in 1991 and, by doing so, recognises children's rights to expression and receiving information.

ORGANISATIONAL RESPONSIBILITIES

Statutory Duties to Co-operate & Safeguard & Promote Welfare of Children

Local Authority Duty to Promote Cooperation [s.10 CA 2004]

- S.10 Children Act 2004 requires each local authority to make arrangements to promote cooperation between the authority, each of the authority's relevant partners and such other persons or bodies working with children in the local authority's area as the authority considers appropriate.

- The arrangements are to be made with a view to improving the wellbeing of all children in the authority's area – which includes protection from harm or neglect alongside other outcomes. The local authority's partners and respective legislative duties are tabulated below.

Bodies & individuals covered by key duties	s.10 CA 2004 duty to co-operate	s.11 CA 2004 duty to safeguard & promote welfare	S.175 EA 2002 duty to safeguard & promote welfare & regulations	s.13 CA 2004 statutory partners in LSCBs	s.27 CA 1989 help with children in need	s.47 CA 1989 help with enquiries about significant harm
Local authorities & District Councils	✗	✗		✗	✗	✗
Local Policing Body	✗	✗				✗
Chief officer of Police	✗	✗		✗		✗
Local Probation Board	✗	✗		✗		
Secretary of State re Probation Service's functions under ss.2,3 OMA 2007	✗	✗		✗		
Providers of probation services under s.3(2) OMA 2007 to act as relevant partner of a local authority	✗	✗		✗		
British Transport Police		✗				
UK Border Agency		✗ (s.55 BCIA 2009)				
Prison or Secure Training Centre		✗		✗ (ordinarily detaining children)		
Youth offending Services	✗	✗		✗		

Bodies & individuals covered by key duties	s.10 CA 2004 duty to co-operate	s.11 CA 2004 duty to safeguard & promote welfare	S.175 EA 2002 duty to safeguard & promote welfare & regulations	s.13 CA 2004 statutory partners in LSCBs	s.27 CA 1989 help with children in need	s.47 CA 1989 help with enquiries about significant harm
NHS Commissioning Board	✗	✗		✗	✗	✗
Clinical Commissioning Groups	✗	✗		✗	✗	✗
NHS Trusts & Foundation Trusts		✗		✗	✗	✗
Cafcass				✗		
Maintained schools	✗ (inc. non-maintained specials)		✗			
FE colleges	✗		✗			
Independent schools	✗		✗ (via regs under s.157 Education Act 2002)			
Academies & Free Schools	✗		✗ (via regulations under s.157 Education Act 2002)			
Contracted services inc. those provided by voluntary organisations		✗	✗			

Duty to Ensure Functions Are Discharged with Regard to the Need to Safeguard & Promote Welfare of Children [s.11 CA 2004]

■ The following organisations have a duty under s.11 Children Act 2004 to 'ensure that their functions are discharged with regard to the need to safeguard and promote the welfare of children:

- Local authorities and district councils that provide children's services, which includes children's and adult social care services, early years and childcare, education services, public health, housing, sport, culture and leisure services, licensing authorities, youth services
- NHS organisations – the NHS Commissioning Board and clinical commissioning groups, NHS Trusts and NHS Foundation Trusts
- Police, including police and crime commissioners and the chief officer of each Police force in England (and the Mayor's Office for Policing and Crime in London)
- British Transport Police
- Probation Service
- Governors/Directors of Prisons and Young Offender Institutions
- Directors of Secure Training Centres and
- Youth Offending Teams/Services

■ These organisations should have in place arrangements that reflect the importance of safeguarding and promoting the welfare of children, including:

- A clear line of accountability for commissioning and/or providing services designed to safeguard and promote the welfare of children
- A senior board-level lead to take leadership responsibility for the organisation's safeguarding arrangements
- A culture of listening to children and taking account of their wishes and feelings both in individual decisions and the development of services
- Arrangements which set out clearly the processes for sharing relevant information with other professionals and with the LSCB
- A designated professional lead (or, for health provider organisations, named professionals) for safeguarding; their role is to support other professionals in their agencies to recognise and respond to the possible abuse and neglect of a child or young person; designated professional roles should always be explicitly defined in job descriptions' professionals should be given sufficient time, funding, supervision and support to fulfil their child welfare and safeguarding responsibilities effectively
- Safe recruitment practices for individuals whom the organisation will permit to work regularly with children, including policies on when to obtain a criminal record check
- Appropriate supervision and support for staff, including undertaking safeguarding training (employer are responsible for ensuring

competence, and an environment in which staff feel able to raise concerns; a mandatory induction to role should be provided)

- Clear policies in line with those from the LSCB for dealing with allegations against people who work with children e.g. about behaviour that has or may have harmed a child, possibly committed a criminal offences against or related to a child or behaved toward a child/ren in a way that indicates they may pose a risk of harm to children

Local Authority Designated Officer (LADO)

- County and Unitary local authorities should have a local authority designated officer (LADO) to be involved in the management and oversight of individual cases of allegations against people who work with children.

- The LADO should provide advice and guidance to employers and voluntary organisation, liaising with Police and other agencies and monitoring the progress of cases to ensure that they are dealt with as quickly as possible, consistent with a thorough and fair process

- Any allegation should be reported immediately to a senior manager within the organisation. The LADO should also be informed within 1 working day of all allegations that come to an employer's attention or that are made directly to the Police.

- If an organisation removes an individual (paid worker or unpaid volunteer) from work such as looking after children (or would have, had the person not left first) because the person poses a risk of harm to children, the organisation must make a referral to the Disclosure and Barring Service. It is an offence to fail to make a referral without good reason.

Individual Organisational Responsibilities

■ In addition to the s.11 duties outlined on previous pages, further safeguarding duties are also placed on individual organisations through other legislation.

Schools & Colleges

■ S.175 Education Act 2002 places a duty on local authorities (in relation to their education functions and governing bodies of maintained schools and further education institutions, which include sixth-form colleges) to exercise their functions with a view to safeguarding and promoting the welfare of children who are pupils at a school, or who are students under 18 years of age attending further education institutions.

■ The same duty applies to independent schools (which include Academies and free schools) by virtue of regulations made under s.157 of the same Act.

■ In order to fulfil their duty under ss.157 and 175 Education Act 2002, all educational settings to whom the duty applies should have in place the s.11 arrangements set out above. In addition schools should have regard to specific guidance given by the Secretary of State under ss.157 and 175 Education Act 2002 i.e. Safeguarding Children and Safer Recruitment in Education (January 2007) and Dealing with allegations of abuse against teachers

and other staff (October 2012) both through
www.education.gov.uk

Early Years & Education

- Early years providers have a duty under s.40
  Childcare Act 2006 to comply with the welfare
  requirements of the Early Years Foundation Stage, see
  The Welfare Requirements of the Early Years
  Foundation Stage at www.education.gov.uk.

- Early Years providers must ensure that:

  - Staff complete safeguarding training that
    enables them to recognise signs of potential
    abuse and neglect; and
  - They have a practitioner who is designated to
    take lead responsibility for safeguarding children
    within each early years setting and who should
    liaise with local statutory Children's Services
    agencies as appropriate; this lead must also
    complete child protection training

Health Services

- Health professionals including GPs, health visitors,
  school nurses and those working in maternity, child
  and adolescent mental health, adult mental health,
  alcohol and drug services and unscheduled care
  settings – are in a strong position to identify and,
  when appropriate, support. This includes
  understanding risk factors, communicating effectively
  with children and families, liaising with other

agencies, assessing needs and capacity, responding to those needs and contributing to multi-agency assessments and reviews.

■ All staff working in healthcare settings including those who predominantly treat adults should receive training to ensure they attain the competencies appropriate to their role and follow relevant guidance e.g. Safeguarding Children & Young People: roles and competencies for health care staff 2010, Looked after children: Knowledge, skills and competencies of health care staff RCN & RCPH 2012 both at www.rcph.ac.uk/and Protecting Children & Young People: the responsibilities of all doctors GMC 2012 at www.gmc-uk.org/

■ The NHS Commissioning Board will be responsible for ensuring that the health commissioning system as a whole is working effectively to safeguard and promote the welfare of children. It will also be accountable for the services it directly commissions.

■ The NHS Commissioning Board will also lead and define improvement in safeguarding practice and outcomes and should ensure that there are effective mechanisms for LSCBs and Health & Wellbeing Boards to raise concerns about the engagement and leadership of the local NHS. Further guidance may be found at www.commissioningboard.nhs.uk

■ Clinical commissioning groups (CCGs) will be the major commissioners of local health services. The CCG should employ, or have in place a contractual agreement to secure the expertise of, designated professionals, i.e. designated doctors and nurses for safeguarding children and for looked after children (and designated paediatricians for unexpected deaths in childhood). Designated professionals are a vital source of advice to the CCG, the local authority and the LSCB, and advice and support for other health professionals.

■ In some areas there will be more than one CCG per local authority and LSCB area, and CCGs may want to consider developing 'lead' or 'hosting' arrangements for their designated professional team, or a clinical network arrangement.

■ All providers of NHS-funded health services – NHS Trusts, NHS Foundation Trusts and public, voluntary sector and social enterprises should identify a named doctor and a named nurse (and a named midwife if the organisation provides maternity services) for safeguarding.

■ In the case of NHS Direct (now the 111 Service), ambulance trusts and independent providers, this should be a named professional. GP practices should have a lead and a deputy lead for safeguarding who should work closely with named GPs.

■ Named professionals have a key role in promoting good practice within an agency, providing advice and expertise for colleagues, and ensuring safeguarding training is in place. They should work closely with the agency's safeguarding lead and the LSCB.

Police

▪ Under s.1(8)(h) Police Reform & Social Responsibility Act 2011 the 'police and crime commissioner' must hold the chief constable to account for the exercise of duties in relation to safeguarding children as set out in ss.10 and 11 Children Act 2004.

▪ All police officers, and other police employees such as 'police community support officers', are well placed to identify early when a child's welfare is at risk and when s/he may need protection from harm. Children have the right to the full protection offered by the criminal law.

▪ In addition to identifying when a child may be a victim of a crime, police officers should be aware of the effect of other incidents which might pose safeguarding risks to children and where officers should pay particular attention. For example, an officer attending a domestic abuse incident should be aware of the effect of such behaviour on any children in the household.

▪ Children who are encountered as offenders, or alleged offenders, are entitled to the same safeguards and protection as any other child and due regard should be given to their welfare at all times.

▪ Police can hold important information about children who may be suffering, or likely to suffer, significant harm, as well as those who cause such harm. They should always share this information with other organisations where this is necessary to protect children. Similarly, they can expect other organisations to share information to enable the police to carry out their duties.

■ Offences committed against children can be particularly sensitive and usually require Police to work with other organisations such as Children's Social Care. All Police Services should have officers trained in child abuse investigation.

■ Police have emergency powers under s.46 Children Act 1989 to enter premises and remove a child to ensure immediate protection. This power can be used if the Police have reasonable cause to believe a child is suffering or is likely to suffer significant harm. Police emergency powers can help in emergencies but should be used only when necessary. Whenever possible, the decision to remove a child from a parent or carer should be made by a court.

Adult Social Care Services

■ Local authorities provide services to adults who are responsible for children who may be in need. These services are subject to the s.11 duties outlined above.

■ When staff are providing services to adults they should ask whether there are children in the family and consider whether the children need help or protection from harm.

■ Children may be at greater risk of harm or be in need of additional help in families where the adults have mental health problems, misuse substances or alcohol, are in violent relationships or have complex needs or have learning difficulties.

▪ Adults with parental responsibilities for disabled children have a right to a separate carer's assessment under the Carers (Recognition and Services) Act 1995 and the Carers and Disabled Children Act 2000. The results of this assessment must be taken into account when deciding what services, if any, will be provided under the Children Act 1989.

Housing Authorities

▪ Housing and homelessness staff in local authorities, and others such as environmental health officers, may become aware of conditions that could have an adverse impact on children. Under Part 1 of the Housing Act 2004, authorities must take account of the impact of health and safety hazards in housing on vulnerable occupants, including children, when deciding on the action to be taken by landlords to improve conditions.

▪ Housing authorities also have an important role to play in safeguarding vulnerable young people, including those who are pregnant or leaving care.

British Transport Police (BTP)

▪ In its role as the national Police for the railways the BTP can play an important role in safeguarding and promoting the welfare of children, especially in identifying and supporting children who have run away or who are truanting from school.

- The BTP must carry out its duties in accordance with its legislative powers, including removing a child to a suitable place using their protection powers under the Children Act 1989 and removal of children truanting from school under the Crime and Disorder Act 1998. This includes appointment of a designated independent officer for a child taken into police protection.

Prison Service

- The Prison Service has a responsibility to identify prisoners who pose a risk of harm to children. If an individual has been identified as presenting a risk of harm −see HMP *Public Protection Manual www. justice.gov.uk/guidance/prison-probation-and-rehabilitation/public-protection-manual* the relevant prison establishment:

  - Should inform Children's Social Care of the offender's reception to prison and subsequent transfers and of the release address of the offender and,
  - Should notify the relevant Probation trust in the case of offenders who have been sentenced to 12 months or more (Police should also be notified of the release address) and
  - May prevent or restrict a prisoner's contact with children; decisions on the level of contact, if any, should be based on a multi-agency risk

assessment which will draw on relevant information held by Police, Probation, Prison and local authority Children's Social Care – see chapter 2 of the HM Prison Service Public Protection Manual cited above.

Probation Service

- Probation Trusts are primarily responsible for providing reports to courts and working with adult offenders in the community and in the transition from custody to community so as to reduce their risk of offending.

- Staff are well placed to identify offenders who pose a risk of harm to children, as well as children who may be at heightened risk of involvement in (or exposure to) criminal or anti-social behaviour and of other poor outcomes due to the offending behaviours of parent/carer.

- When an adult offender is assessed as presenting a risk of serious harm to children, the offender manager should develop a risk management plan and supervision plan that contains a specific objective to manage and reduce the risk of harm to children.

- In preparing a sentence plan, offender managers should consider how planned interventions might bear on parental responsibilities and whether the planned interventions could contribute to improved outcomes for children known to be in an existing relationship with the offender.

Secure Estate for Children

■ Governors, managers and directors of the following secure establishments are subject to the s.11 duties set out above:

- Secure training centres (STCs)
- Young offender institutions (YOIs)
- Accommodation provided by or on behalf of a local authority for the purpose of restricting the liberty of children/young people
- Accommodation provided for that purpose under s.82(5) Children Act 1989 and
- Such other accommodation or descriptions of accommodation as the Secretary of State may by order specify

■ Each centre holding those aged under 18 should have in place an annually reviewed safeguarding children policy designed to promote and safeguard the welfare of children and covering issues such as child protection, risk of harm, restraint, recruitment and information sharing.

■ A safeguarding manager should be appointed to be responsible for implementation of this policy.

■ Detailed guidance on these matters may be found in Prison Service Instruction (PSI) 08/2012 *Care & Management of Young People.*

Youth Offending Team (YOTs)

■ As multi-agency teams responsible for the supervision of children and young people subject to pre-court interventions and statutory court disposals YOTs are well placed to identify children known to relevant organisations as being most at risk of offending, and to undertake work to prevent them offending.

■ YOTs should also have a lead officer responsible for ensuring safeguarding is at the forefront of their work.

■ Under s.38 Crime and Disorder Act 1998, local authorities must, within the delivery of youth justice services, ensure the 'provision of persons to act as appropriate adults to safeguard the interests of children and young persons detained or questioned by police officers'.

UK Border Agency (UKBA)

■ S.55 Borders, Citizenship and Immigration Act 2009 places upon the UKBA a duty to take account of the need to safeguard and promote the welfare of children in discharging its functions.

■ Statutory guidance '*Arrangements to Safeguard and Promote Children's Welfare in the United Kingdom Border Agency*' www.ukba.homeoffice.gov.uk/sitecontent/documents/policyandlaw/legislation/bci-act1/sets out the agency's responsibilities.

Children & Family Court Advisory & Support Service (Cafcass)

- The responsibility of Cafcass is to safeguard and promote the welfare of individual children who are the subject of family proceedings by providing independent social work advice to the court.

- A Cafcass officer has a statutory right in public law cases to make use of local authority records relating to the child concerned and any application under the Children Act 1989. That power also extends to other records that relate to the child and the wider functions of the local authority, or records held by an authorised body that relate to that child.

- When a Cafcass officer has been appointed by the court as a child's guardian and the matter before the court relates to specified proceeding s/he should be invited to all formal planning meetings convened by the local authority in respect of the child. This includes statutory reviews of children who are accommodated or looked after, child protection conferences, and relevant adoption panel meetings.

Armed Services

- Local authorities have the statutory responsibility for safeguarding and promoting the welfare of the children of service families in the UK.

- In discharging their responsibilities:

■ Local authorities should ensure that the Soldiers, Sailors, Airmen and Families Association Forces Help, the British Forces Social Work Service or the Naval Personal and Family Services is made aware of any service child who is the subject of a child protection plan and whose family is about to move overseas

■ Each local authority with a United States base in its area should establish liaison arrangements with the base commander and relevant staff; the requirements of English child welfare legislation should be explained clearly to the US authorities, so that local authorities can fulfil their statutory duty

Voluntary & Private Sectors

■ Voluntary organisations and private sector providers play an important role in delivering services to children. They should have the arrangements under s.11 Children Act 2004 in place in the same way as organisations in the public sector, and need to work effectively with the LSCB.

■ Paid and volunteer staff need to be aware of their responsibilities for safeguarding and promoting the welfare of children, how they should respond to child protection concerns and make a referral to Children's Social Care or the Police if necessary.

Faith Organisations

■ Churches, other places of worship and Faith-based organisations provide a wide range of activities for children and have an important role in safeguarding children and supporting families.

- Like other organisations who work with children they need to have appropriate arrangements in place to safeguard and promote the welfare of children, as described for other organisations.

ASSESSING NEED & PROVIDING HELP

Early Help

- Providing early help is more effective in promoting the welfare of children than reacting later. Early help means providing support as soon as a problem emerges, at any point in a child's life, from the foundation years through to the teenage years.

- Effective early help relies upon local agencies working together to:
  - Identify children and families who would benefit from early help
  - Undertake an assessment of their need
  - Provide targeted early help services to address the assessed needs of a child and family which focuses on activity to significantly improve the outcomes for the child

Identifying Children & Families who Would Benefit from Early Help

- Local agencies should have in place effective ways to identify emerging problems and potential unmet needs for individual children and families.

- This requires all professionals, including those in universal services and those providing services to adults with children, to understand their role in identifying emerging problems and to share information with other professionals to support early identification and assessment.

■ Local Safeguarding Children Boards (LSCBs) should monitor and evaluate the effectiveness of training, including multi-agency training, for all professionals in the area. Training should cover how to identify and respond early to the needs of all vulnerable children, including: unborn children; babies; older children; young carers; disabled children; and those who are in secure settings.

■ Professionals should, in particular, be alert to the potential need for early help for a child who:

- Is disabled and has specific additional needs
- Has special educational needs
- Is a young carer
- Is showing signs of engaging in anti-social or criminal behaviour
- Is in a family circumstance presenting challenges for the child, such as substance abuse, adult mental health, domestic violence and/or
- Is showing early signs of abuse and/or neglect

■ Professionals working in universal services have a responsibility to identify the symptoms and triggers of abuse and neglect, to share that information and work together to provide children/young people with the help they need. Practitioners need to continue to develop their knowledge and skills in this area and should have access to training to identify and respond early to abuse and neglect, and to the latest research showing what types of interventions are the most effective.

Effective Assessment of the Need for Early Help

■ Local agencies should work together to put processes in place for the effective assessment of the needs of individual children who may benefit from early help services.

■ Children and families may need support from a wide range of local agencies. When a child and family would benefit from coordinated support from more than one agency e.g. education, health, housing, police, there should be an inter-agency assessment.

■ These early help assessments, such as the use of the Common Assessment Framework (CAF), should identify what help the child and family require to prevent needs escalating to a point where intervention would be needed via a statutory assessment under the Children Act 1989.

■ The early help assessment should be undertaken by a lead professional who should provide support to the child and family, act as an advocate on their behalf and coordinate the delivery of support services.

■ The lead professional role could be undertaken by a General Practitioner (GP), family support worker, teacher, health visitor and/or special educational needs coordinator. Decisions about who should be the lead professional should be taken on a case by case basis and should be informed by the child and their family.

■ For an early help assessment to be effective:

- The assessment should be undertaken with the agreement of the child and parents/carers; it should involve the child and family as well as all the professionals who are working with them
- A teacher, GP, health visitor, early years' worker or other professional should be able to discuss concerns they may have about a child and family with a social worker in the local authority; Children's Social Care should set out the process for how this will happen and
- If parents and/or the child do not consent to an early help assessment, the lead professional should make a judgement as to whether, without help, the needs of the child will escalate; if so, a referral into Children's Social Care may be necessary

■ If at any time it is considered that the child may be a child in need as defined in the Children Act 1989, or that the child has suffered significant harm or is likely to do so, a referral should be made immediately to local authority children's social care. This referral can be made by any professional.

Provision of Effective Early Help Services

■ The early help assessment carried out for an individual child and family should be clear about the action to be taken and services to be provided (including any relevant timescales for the assessment) and aim to ensure that early help services are coordinated and not delivered in a piecemeal way.

■ Local areas should have a range of effective, evidence-based services in place to address assessed needs early. The early help on offer should draw upon the local assessment of need and the latest evidence of the effectiveness of early help and early intervention programmes.

■ In addition to high quality support in universal services, specific local early help services will typically include family and parenting programmes, assistance with health issues and help for problems relating to drugs, alcohol and domestic violence.

■ Services may also focus on improving family functioning and building the family's own capability to solve problems; this should be done within a structured, evidence-based framework involving regular review to ensure that real progress is being made. Some of these services may be delivered to parents but should always be evaluated to demonstrate the impact they are having on the outcomes for the child.

Accessing Help & Services

■ The provision of early help services should form part of a continuum of help and support to respond to the different levels of need of individual children and families.

■ When need is relatively low-level individual services and universal services may be able to take swift action. For other emerging needs a range of early help services may be required, coordinated through an early help assessment, as set out above.

- If there are more complex needs, help may be provided under s.17 Children Act 1989 (children in need). When there are child protection concerns (reasonable cause to *suspect* a child is suffering or likely to suffer significant harm) Children's Social Care services must make enquiries and decide if any action must be taken under s.47 Children Act 1989.

- It is important that there are clear criteria for taking action and providing help across this full continuum. Having clear thresholds for action which are understood by all professionals, and applied consistently, should ensure that services are commissioned effectively and that the right help is given to the child at the right time.

- The LSCB should agree with the local authority and its partners the levels for the different types of assessment and services to be commissioned and delivered. Children's Social Care has the responsibility for clarifying the process for referrals.

- The LSCB should publish a 'threshold document' that includes the:

  - Process for the early help assessment and type and level of early help services to be provided
  - Criteria, including the level of need, for when a case should be referred to Children's Social Care for assessment and for statutory services under s.17 (children in need), s.47 (reasonable cause to

suspect children suffering or likely to suffer significant harm), s.31(Care Orders) and s.20 (duty to accommodate a child) Children Act 1989.

- Anyone who has concerns about a child's welfare should make a referral to Children's Social Care. Referrals may come from: children, teachers, a GP, the police, health visitors, family members and members of the public.

- Within local authorities, Children's Social Care should act as the principal point of contact for welfare concerns relating to children. As well as clear protocols for professionals working with children, contact details should be signposted clearly so that children, parents and other family members are aware of who they can contact if they require advice and/or support.

- When professionals refer a child, they should include any information they have on the child's developmental needs and the capacity of the child's parents or carers to meet those needs. This information may be included in any assessment, including the early help assessment, which may have been carried out prior to a referral to Children's Social Care.

- When an early help assessment has already been undertaken it should be used to support a referral to Children's Social Care though this is *not* a prerequisite for making a referral.

- Feedback should be given by Children's Social Care to the referrer on the decisions taken. When appropriate, feedback should include reasons why a case may not meet the statutory threshold for assessment and suggestions for other sources of more suitable support.

Information sharing

- Effective sharing of information between professionals and local agencies is essential for effective identification, assessment and service provision.

- Early sharing of information is the key to providing effective early help where there are emerging problems. At the other end of the continuum, sharing information can be essential to put in place effective child protection services. Serious Case Reviews (SCRs) have shown how poor information sharing has contributed to the deaths or serious injuries of children.

- Fears about sharing information cannot be allowed to stand in the way of the need to promote the welfare and protect the safety of children.

- To ensure effective safeguarding arrangements:

  - All organisations should have arrangements in place which set out clearly the processes and the principles for sharing information between each other, with other professionals and with the LSCB
  - No professional should assume that someone else will pass on information which s/he thinks may be critical to keeping a child safe; if a professional has concerns about a child's welfare and believes s/he is suffering or likely to suffer harm, s/he should share the information with Children's Social Care

- *Information Sharing: Guidance for practitioners and managers* (2008) supports frontline practitioners, working in child or adult services, who have to make decisions about sharing personal information on a case by case basis -see the DfE guidance on information sharing at www.education.gov.uk .
- The guidance can be used to supplement local guidance and encourage good practice in information sharing.

Assessments under the Children Act 1989

Options for Statutory Assessments

- Under the Children Act 1989, local authorities are required to provide services for children in need for the purposes of safeguarding and promoting their welfare. Local authorities undertake assessments of the needs of individual children to determine what services to provide and action to take.

- A child in need is defined under the Children Act 1989 as a child who is 'unlikely to achieve or maintain a satisfactory level of health or development, or their health and development will be significantly impaired, without the provision of services; or a child who is disabled'

- In these cases, assessments by a social worker are carried out under s.17 Children Act 1989. Children in need may be assessed under s.17 in relation to their special educational needs, disabilities, or as a carer, or because they have committed a crime.

- The process for assessment should also be used for children whose parents are in prison and for asylum seeking children. When assessing children in need and providing services, specialist assessments may be required and, where possible, should be coordinated so that the child and family experience a coherent process and a single plan of action.

▪ Concerns about maltreatment may be the reason for a referral to Children's Social Care or concerns may arise during the course of providing services to the child and family.

▪ In these circumstances, Children's Social Care must initiate enquiries to find out what is happening to the child and whether protective action is required. Local authorities, with the help of other organisations as appropriate, also have a duty to make enquiries under s.47 Children Act 1989 if they have reasonable cause to *suspect* that a child is suffering, or is likely to suffer, significant harm, to enable them to decide whether they should take any action to safeguard and promote the child's welfare. There may be a need for immediate protection whilst the assessment is carried out.

▪ Some children in need may require accommodation because there is no one who has parental responsibility for them, or because they are alone or abandoned. Under s.20 Children Act 1989, the local authority has a duty to accommodate such children in need in its area.

▪ Following an application under s.31A Children Act 1989, if a child is the subject of a Care Order, the local authority, as a corporate parent, must assess the child's needs and draw up a care plan which sets out the services which will be provided to meet the child's identified needs.

Purpose of Assessment

■ Whatever legislation a child is assessed under, the purpose of the assessment is always to:

- Gather important information about a child and family
- Analyse their needs and/or the nature and level of any risk and harm being suffered by the child
- Decide whether the child is a child in need (s.17) and/or is suffering or likely to suffer significant harm (s.47)
- Provide support to address those needs to improve the child's outcomes to make her/him safe

■ Assessment should be a dynamic process, which analyses and responds to the changing nature and level of need and/or risk faced by the child. A good assessment will monitor and record the impact of any services delivered to the child and family and review the help being delivered.

■ Whilst services may be delivered to a parent or carer, the assessment should be focused on the needs of the child and on the impact any services are having on the child.

■ Good assessments support professionals to understand whether a child has needs relating to her/his care or a disability and/or is suffering, or likely to suffer, significant harm.

■ The specific needs of disabled children and young carers should be given sufficient recognition and priority in the assessment process. Further guidance can be accessed at *Safeguarding Disabled Children – Practice Guidance* (2009) at www.education.gov.uk and *Recognised, valued and supported: Next steps for the Carers Strategy* (2010) at www.gov.uk

■ Practitioners should be rigorous in assessing and monitoring children at risk of neglect to ensure they are adequately safeguarded over time. They should act decisively to protect the child by initiating Care Proceedings when existing interventions are insufficient.

■ When a child becomes looked after the assessment will be the baseline for work with the family. Any needs which have been identified should be addressed before decisions are made about the child's return home.

■ An assessment by a social worker is required before the child returns home under the Care Planning, Placement and Case Review (England) Regulations 2010. This will provide evidence of whether the necessary improvements have been made to ensure the child's safety when they return home.

Principles & Parameters of a Good Assessment

■ High quality assessments are:

- Child centred and if there is a conflict of interest, decisions should be made in the child's best interests
- Rooted in child development and informed by evidence
- Focused on action and outcomes for children
- Holistic in approach, addressing the child's needs within their family and wider community
- Able to ensure equality of opportunity
- Able to involve children and families
- Able to build on strengths as well as identifying difficulties
- Integrated in approach
- A continuing process not an event
- Likely to lead to action, including the provision and review of services and
- Transparent and open to challenge

■ Research has shown that taking a systematic approach to enquiries using a conceptual model is the best way to deliver a comprehensive assessment for all children.

■ A good assessment is one which investigates the following three domains, set out in the Assessment Framework diagram below:

- The child's developmental needs, including whether s/he is suffering or likely to suffer significant harm
- Parent/carer's capacity to respond to those need and

- The impact and influence of wider family, community and environmental circumstances

■ The interaction of these domains requires careful investigation during the assessment. The aim is to reach a judgement about the nature and level of needs and/or risks that the child may be facing within their family.

■ It is important that:

- Information is gathered and recorded systematically
- Information is checked and discussed with the child and parents/carers when appropriate
- Differences in views about information are recorded and
- The impact of what is happening to the child is clearly identified

Assessment Framework

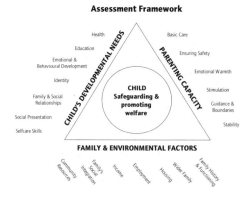

233

■ Assessments for some children – including young carers, children with special educational needs (who may require statements of SEN or Education Health and Care Plans, unborn children where there are concerns, asylum seeking children, children in hospital, disabled children, children with specific communication needs, children considered at risk of gang activity, children who are in the youth justice system – will require particular care.

■ Young carers are also entitled to request a separate carer's assessment under the Carers (Recognition and Services) Act 1995 and, if they are over 16 years, under the Carers and Disabled Act 2000.

■ When a child has other assessments it is important that these are coordinated so that the child does not become lost between the different agencies involved and their different procedures.

Focusing on the Needs & Views of the Child

■ Every assessment should be child centred. When there is a conflict between the needs of the child and parents/carers, decisions should be made in the child's best interests.

■ Each child who has been referred to Children's Social Care should have an individual assessment to respond to her/his needs and to understand the impact of any parental behaviour on the individual. Local authorities have to give due regard to a child's age and understanding when determining what (if any) services to provide under s.17 Children Act 1989, and before making decisions about action to be taken to protect individual children under s.47 of the Children Act 1989.

- Every assessment must be informed by the views of the child as well as the family. Children should, wherever possible, be seen alone and Children's Social Care has a duty to ascertain the child's wishes and feelings regarding the provision of services to be delivered (s.17 Children Act 1989, amended by s.53 Children Act 2004). It is important to understand the resilience of the individual child when planning appropriate services.

- Every assessment should reflect the unique characteristics of the child within their family and community context. The Children Act 1989 promotes the view that all children and their parents should be considered as individuals and that family structures, culture, religion, ethnic origins and other characteristics should be respected.

- Every assessment should draw together relevant information gathered from the child and their family and from relevant professionals including teachers, early years workers, health professionals, Police and Adults Social Care.

- A high quality assessment is one in which evidence is built and revised throughout the process. A social worker may arrive at a judgement early in the case but this may need to be revised as the case progresses and further information comes to light. It is a characteristic of skilled practice that social workers revisit their assumptions in the light of new evidence and take action to revise their decisions in the best interests of the individual child.

■ The aim is to use all the information to identify difficulties and risk factors as well as developing a picture of strengths and protective factors.

Developing a Clear Analysis

■ The social worker should analyse all the information gathered from the enquiry stage of the assessment to decide the nature and level of the child's needs and the level of risk, if any, they may be facing.

■ The social work manager should challenge the social worker's assumptions as part of this process. An informed decision should be taken on the nature of any action required and which services should be provided. Social workers, their managers and other professionals should be mindful of the requirement to understand the level of need and risk in a family from the child's perspective and ensure action or commission services which will have maximum impact on the child's life.

■ No system can fully eliminate risk. Understanding risk involves judgement and balance. To manage risks, social workers and other professionals should make decisions with the best interests of the child in mind, informed by the evidence available and underpinned by knowledge of child development.

■ Critical reflection through supervision should strengthen the analysis in each assessment.

■ Social workers, their managers and other professionals should always consider the plan from the child's perspective. A desire to think the best of adults and to hope they can overcome their difficulties should not trump the need to rescue children from chaotic, neglectful and abusive homes. Social workers and managers should always reflect the latest research on the impact of neglect and abuse when analysing the level of need and risk faced by the child. This should be reflected in the case recording.

■ Assessment is a dynamic and continuous process which should build upon the history of every individual case, responding to the impact of any previous services and analysing what further action might be needed. Social workers should build on this with help from other professionals from the moment that a need is identified.

■ Decision points and review points involving the child and family and relevant professionals should be used to keep the assessment on track. This is to ensure that help is given in a timely and appropriate way and that the impact of this help is analysed and evaluated in terms of the improved outcomes and welfare of the child.

Focusing on Outcomes

■ Every assessment should be focused on outcomes, deciding which services and support to provide to deliver improved welfare for the child.

■ When the outcome of the assessment is continued Children's Social Care involvement, the social worker and manager should agree a plan of action with other professionals and discuss this with the child and their family. The plan should set out what services are to be delivered, and what actions are to be undertaken, by whom and for what purpose.

■ Many services provided will be for parents or carers. The plan should reflect this and set clear measurable outcomes for the child and expectations for the parents, with measurable, reviewable actions for them.

■ The plan should be reviewed regularly to analyse whether sufficient progress has been made to meet the child's needs and on the level of risk faced by the child.

■ This will be important for neglect cases where parents and carers can make small improvements. The test should be whether any improvements in adult behaviour are sufficient and sustained.

■ Social workers and their managers should consider the need for further action and record their decisions. The review points should be agreed by the social worker with other professionals and with the child and family to continue evaluating the impact of any change on the welfare of the child.

■ Effective professional supervision can play a critical role in ensuring a clear focus on a child's welfare. Supervision should support professionals to reflect critically on the impact of their decisions on the child and their family.

■ The social worker and their manager should review the plan for the child. Together they should ask whether the help given is leading to a significant positive change for the child and whether the pace of that change is appropriate for the child.

■ Any professional working with vulnerable children should always have access to a manager to talk through their concerns and judgements affecting the welfare of the child. Assessment should remain an ongoing process, with the impact of services informing future decisions around action.

Timeliness

■ The timeliness of an assessment is a critical element of its quality and the outcomes for the child. The speed with which an assessment is carried out after a child's case has been referred into Children's Social Care should be determined by the needs of the individual child and the nature and level of any risk of harm faced by the child. This will require judgements to be made by the social worker in discussion with their manager on each individual case.

■ Within 1 working day of a referral being received, a local authority social worker should make a decision about the type of response that is required and acknowledge receipt to the referrer.

■ For children who are in need of immediate protection, action must be taken by the social worker, or the Police or NSPCC if removal is required, as soon as possible after the referral has been made to local authority children's social care (ss.44 and 46 respectively Children Act 1989).

■ The maximum timeframe for the assessment to conclude, such that it is possible to reach a decision on next steps, should be no longer than 45 working days from the point of referral. If, in discussion with a child and their family and other professionals, an assessment exceeds 45 working days the social worker should record the reasons for exceeding the time limit.

■ Whatever the timescale for assessment, if particular needs are identified at any stage of the assessment, social workers should not wait until the assessment reaches a conclusion before commissioning services to support the child and their family. In some cases the needs of the child will mean that a quick assessment will be required.

■ The assessment of neglect cases can be difficult. Neglect can fluctuate both in level and duration. A child's welfare can, for example, improve following input from services or a change in circumstances and review, but then deteriorate once support is removed. Professionals should be wary of being too optimistic. Timely and decisive action is critical to ensure that children are not left in neglectful homes.

- It is the responsibility of the social worker to make clear to children and families how the assessment will be carried out and when they can expect a decision on next steps.

- To facilitate the shift to an assessment process which brings continuity and consistency for children and families, there will no longer be a requirement to conduct separate initial and core assessments. Local authorities should determine their local assessment processes through a local protocol.

Local Protocols for Assessment

■ Local authorities, with their partners, should develop and publish local protocols for assessment. A local protocol should set out clear arrangements for how cases will be managed once a child is referred into Children's Social Care and be consistent with the requirements of *Working Together to Safeguard Children* 2013. The detail of each protocol will be led by the local authority in discussion with their partners and agreed with the relevant LSCB.

■ The local authority is publicly accountable for this protocol and all organisations and agencies have a responsibility to understand their local protocol, which should:

- Ensure that assessments are timely, transparent and proportionate to the needs of individual children and their families
- Set out how the needs of disabled children, young carers and children involved in the youth justice system will be addressed in the assessment process
- Clarify how agencies and professionals undertaking assessments and providing services can make contributions
- Clarify how the statutory assessments will be informed by other specialist assessments, such as the assessment for children with special educational needs (Education, Health and Care Plan) and disabled children

- Ensure that any specialist assessments are coordinated so that the child and family experience a joined up assessment process and a single planning process focused on outcomes
- Set out how shared internal review points with other professionals and the child and family will be managed throughout the assessment process
- Set out the process for assessment for children who are returned from care to live with their families
- Seek to ensure that each child and family understands the type of help offered and their own responsibilities, so as to improve the child's outcomes
- Set out the process for challenge by children and families by publishing the complaints procedure
- Require decisions to be recorded in accordance with locally agreed procedures; recording should include information on the child's development so that progress can be monitored to ensure her/his outcomes are improving, thus reducing the need for repeat assessments during Care Proceedings (which can be a major source of delay)

MANAGING INDIVIDUAL CASES

Children's Social Care Response to a Referral

■ Once the referral has been accepted by Children's Social Care the lead professional role falls to a social worker.

■ The social worker should clarify with the referrer, when known, the nature of the concerns and how and why they have arisen.

■ Within 1 working day of a referral being received a local authority social worker should make a decision about the type of response that is required. This will include determining whether:

- The child requires immediate protection and urgent action is required
- The child is in need, and should be assessed under s.17 Children Act 1989
- There is reasonable cause to *suspect* that the child is suffering, or likely to suffer, significant harm, and whether enquires must be made and the child assessed under s.47 Children Act 1989
- Any services are required by the child and family and what type of services and
- Further specialist assessments are required in order to help the local authority to decide what further action to take

■ The child and family must be informed of the action to be taken.

- Children's Social Care should see the child as soon as possible if the decision is taken that the referral requires further assessment.

- When requested to do so by Children's Social Care, professionals from other parts of the local authority such as housing and those in health organisations have a duty to cooperate under s.27 Children Act 1989 by assisting the local authority in carrying out its Children's Social Care functions.

Flow chart 1: Action taken when child referred to Children's Social Care

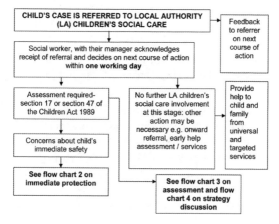

Immediate Protection

■ When there is a risk to the life of a child or a likelihood of serious immediate harm, local authority social workers, Police or NSPCC should use their statutory child protection powers to act immediately.

■ If it is necessary to remove a child from home, a local authority must, wherever possible and unless a child's safety is otherwise at immediate risk, apply for an Emergency Protection Order (EPO).

■ Police powers to remove a child in an emergency should be used only in exceptional circumstances where there is insufficient time to seek an EPO or for reasons relating to the immediate safety of the child.

■ An EPO, made by the court, authorises removal of child and places her/him under the protection of the applicant.

■ When considering whether emergency action is necessary an agency should always consider the needs of other children in the same household or in the household of an alleged perpetrator.

■ The local authority in whose area a child is found in circumstances that require emergency action (the first authority) is responsible for taking emergency action.

■ If the child is looked after by, or subject of a child protection plan in another authority, the first authority must consult the responsible authority. Only when the second local authority explicitly accepts responsibility (to be followed up in writing) is the first authority relieved of its responsibility to take emergency action

Multi-agency Working

- Planned emergency action will normally take place following an immediate strategy discussion.

- Social workers, Police or NSPCC should:

  - Initiate a strategy discussion to discuss planned emergency action; if a single agency has to act immediately, a strategy discussion should take place as soon as possible after action taken
  - See the child (this should be done by a practitioner from the agency taking the emergency action) to decide how best to protect her/him and whether to seek an EPO
  - Whenever possible, obtain legal advice before initiating legal action, in particular when an EPO is being sought

NB. For further guidance on EPOs, see pp.55–65 of VO1.1 Children Act Guidance & Regulations: Court Orders

Flow chart 2: Immediate Protection

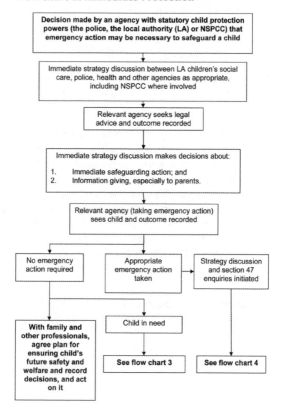

Decision made by an agency with statutory child protection powers (the police, the local authority (LA) or NSPCC) that emergency action may be necessary to safeguard a child

Immediate strategy discussion between LA children's social care, police, health and other agencies as appropriate, including NSPCC where involved

Relevant agency seeks legal advice and outcome recorded

Immediate strategy discussion makes decisions about:

1. Immediate safeguarding action; and
2. Information giving, especially to parents.

Relevant agency (taking emergency action) sees child and outcome recorded

No emergency action required

Appropriate emergency action taken

Strategy discussion and section 47 enquiries initiated

With family and other professionals, agree plan for ensuring child's future safety and welfare and record decisions, and act on it

Child in need

See flow chart 3

See flow chart 4

Assessment of a Child under Children Act 1989

- Following acceptance of a referral by Children's Social Care, a social worker should lead a multi-agency assessment under s.17 Children Act 1989. Local authorities have a duty to ascertain the child's wishes and feelings and take account of them when planning service provision. Assessments should be carried out in a timely manner reflecting the needs of the individual child.

- If Children's Social Care decides to provide services, a multi-agency 'child in need' (CIN) plan should be developed which sets out which agencies will provide which services to the child and family. The plan should set clear measurable outcomes for the child and expectations for the parents. The plan should reflect the positive aspects of the family situation as well as the weaknesses.

- When information gathered during an assessment (which may be very brief) results in the social worker suspecting that the child is suffering or likely to suffer significant harm, the local authority should hold a strategy discussion to enable it to decide, with other agencies, whether to initiate enquiries under s.47 Children Act 1989.

- Assessments should determine whether the child is in need, the nature of any services required and whether any specialist assessments should be undertaken to assist the local authority in its decision making.

■ Social workers should:

- Lead on an assessment and complete it in line with the locally agreed protocol according to the child's needs and within 45 working days from the point of referral into Children's Social Care
- See the child within a timescale that is appropriate to the nature of the concerns expressed at referral, according to an agreed plan
- Conduct interviews with the child and family members, separately and together as appropriate; initial discussions with the child should be conducted in a way that minimises distress to her/him and maximises the likelihood that they will provide accurate and complete information, avoiding leading or suggestive questions
- Record the assessment findings and decisions and next steps following the assessment
- Inform, in writing, all the relevant agencies and the family of their decisions and, if the child is a child in need, of the plan for providing support
- Inform the referrer of what action has been or will be taken

■ Police should assist other agencies to carry out their responsibilities where there are concerns about the child's welfare, whether or not a crime has been committed.

- If a crime has been committed, the police should be informed by the Children's Social Care.

- All involved professionals should:

  - Be involved in the assessment and provide further information about the child and family
  - Agree further action including what services would help the child and family and inform Children's Social Care if any immediate action is required.

Flow chart 3: Action taken for an assessment of a child under the Children Act 1989

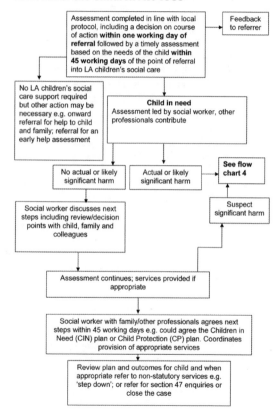

Assessment completed in line with local protocol, including a decision on course of action **within one working day of referral** followed by a timely assessment based on the needs of the child **within 45 working days** of the point of referral into LA children's social care

Feedback to referrer

No LA children's social care support required but other action may be necessary e.g. onward referral for help to child and family; referral for an early help assessment

Child in need
Assessment led by social worker, other professionals contribute

No actual or likely significant harm

Actual or likely significant harm

See flow chart 4

Social worker discusses next steps including review/decision points with child, family and colleagues

Suspect significant harm

Assessment continues; services provided if appropriate

Social worker with family/other professionals agrees next steps within 45 working days e.g. could agree the Children in Need (CIN) plan or Child Protection (CP) plan. Coordinates provision of appropriate services

Review plan and outcomes for child and when appropriate refer to non-statutory services e.g. 'step down'; or refer for section 47 enquiries or close the case

Strategy Discussion

■ Whenever there is reasonable cause to *suspect* that a child is suffering, or is likely to suffer, significant harm there should be a strategy discussion involving Children's Social Care, Police, Health and other bodies such as the referring agency.

■ This might take the form of a multi-agency meeting or phone calls and more than one discussion may be necessary. A strategy discussion can take place following a referral or at any other time, including during the assessment process.

Purpose

■ Children's Social Care should convene a strategy discussion to determine the child's welfare, and plan rapid future action if there is reasonable cause to suspect s/he is suffering, or is likely to suffer, significant harm.

Attendees

■ A social worker, her/his manager, health professionals and a Police representative should, at minimum, be involved. Other relevant professionals will depend on the nature of the individual case but may include:

- The referring professional or agency
- The child's school or nursery; and
- Any health services child or family are receiving

- All attendees should be sufficiently senior to make decisions on behalf of their agencies.

Tasks & Task Allocation

- The discussion should be used to:

  - Share available information
  - Agree the conduct and timing of any criminal investigation;
  - Decide whether enquiries under s.47 Children Act 1989 should be undertaken

- When there are grounds to initiate s.47 enquiries, decisions should be made as to:

  - What further information is needed if an assessment is already underway and how it will be obtained and recorded
  - What immediate and short term action is required to support the child, and who will do what by when and
  - Whether legal action is required

- The timescale for the assessment to reach a decision on next steps should be based upon the needs of the individual child, consistent with the local protocol and certainly no longer than 45 working days from the point of referral into Children's Social Care.

- The principles and parameters for the assessment of children in need as on p.239 should be followed for assessments undertaken under s.47 Children Act 1989.

■ Social workers with their managers should convene the strategy discussion and make sure it:

- Considers the child's welfare and safety, and identifies the level of risk faced by the child
- Decides what information should be shared with the child and family (on the basis information is *not* shared if it might jeopardise a Police investigation or place the child at risk of significant harm)
- Agrees required further action, and who will do what by when, if an EPO is in place or the child is the subject of police powers of protection
- Records agreed decisions in accordance with local recording procedures
- Follows up actions to make sure what was agreed gets done

■ Police should:

- Discuss the basis for any criminal investigation and any relevant processes that other agencies might need to know about, including the timing and methods of evidence gathering and
- Lead the criminal investigation (Children's Social Care has the lead for s.47 enquires and assessment of the child's welfare) where joint enquiries take place

Flow chart 4: Action following a strategy discussion

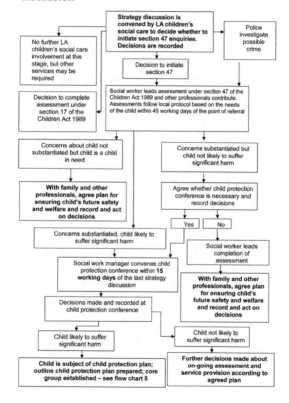

Strategy discussion is convened by LA children's social care to decide whether to initiate section 47 enquiries. Decisions are recorded

Police investigate possible crime

No further LA children's social care involvement at this stage, but other services may be required

Decision to initiate section 47

Social worker leads assessment under section 47 of the Children Act 1989 and other professionals contribute. Assessments follow local protocol based on the needs of the child within 45 working days of the point of referral

Decision to complete assessment under section 17 of the Children Act 1989

Concerns about child not substantiated but child is a child in need

Concerns substantiated but child not likely to suffer significant harm

With family and other professionals, agree plan for ensuring child's future safety and welfare and record and act on decisions

Agree whether child protection conference is necessary and record decisions

Yes   No

Concerns substantiated, child likely to suffer significant harm

Social worker leads completion of assessment

Social work manager convenes child protection conference within 15 working days of the last strategy discussion

With family and other professionals, agree plan for ensuring child's future safety and welfare and record and act on decisions

Decisions made and recorded at child protection conference

Child likely to suffer significant harm

Child not likely to suffer significant harm

Child is subject of child protection plan; outline child protection plan prepared; core group established – see flow chart 5

Further decisions made about on-going assessment and service provision according to agreed plan

Initiating s.47 Enquiries

■ S.47 enquiries are carried out by undertaking or continuing with an assessment in accordance with the guidance in *Working Together to Safeguard Children* 2013 and following the principles and parameters of a good assessment.

■ Local authority social workers have a statutory duty to lead assessments under s.47 Children Act 1989. Police, health professionals, teachers and other relevant professionals should help the local authority in undertaking its enquiries.

Purpose

■ S.47 enquiries are initiated to decide whether and what type of action is required to safeguard and promote the welfare of a child who is suspected of, or likely to be, suffering significant harm.

Task Allocation

■ Social workers with their managers should:

  • Lead the assessment in accordance with *Working Together to Safeguard Children* 2013
  • Carry out enquiries in a way that minimises distress for the child and family
  • See the child who is the subject of concern to ascertain her/his wishes and feelings, assess the child's understanding of her/his situation, assess relationships and circumstances more broadly

- Interview parents and/or caregivers and determine the wider social and environmental factors that might impact on them and their child
- Systematically gather information about the child's and family's history
- Analyse the findings of the assessment and evidence about what interventions are likely to be most effective with other relevant professionals to determine the child's needs and the level of risk of harm faced by the child to inform what help should be provided and act to provide that help
- Follow the guidance set out in *Achieving Best Evidence in Criminal Proceedings: Guidance on interviewing victims and witnesses at www. justice.gov.uk* and guidance on using special measures, if a decision has been made to undertake a joint interview of the child as part of any criminal investigation.

◼ Police should:

- Help other agencies understand the reasons for concerns about the child's safety and welfare
- Decide whether Police investigations reveal grounds for instigating criminal proceedings
- Make available to other professionals any evidence gathered to inform discussions about the child's welfare
- Follow the guidance set out in *Achieving Best Evidence in Criminal Proceedings: Guidance on*

interviewing victims and witnesses, and guidance on using special measures, if a decision has been made to undertake a joint interview of the child as part of the criminal investigations.

■ Health professionals should:

- Undertake appropriate medical tests, examinations or observations, to determine how the child's health or development may be being impaired
- Provide any of a range of specialist assessments e.g. physiotherapists, occupational therapists, speech and language therapists and child psychologists may be involved in specific assessments relating to the child's developmental progress; the lead health practitioner (probably a consultant paediatrician, or possibly the child's GP) may need to request and coordinate these assessments
- Ensure appropriate treatment and follow up health concerns

■ All involved professionals should:

- Contribute to the assessment as required, providing information about the child and family
- Consider whether a joint enquiry/investigation team may need to speak to a child victim without the knowledge of the parent or caregiver

Outcome of s.47 Enquiries

■ Local authority social workers are responsible for deciding how to proceed following s.47 enquiries.

■ If Children's Social Care decides *not* to proceed with a child protection conference, other professionals involved with the child and family have the right, if they have serious concerns that a child's welfare may not otherwise be adequately safeguarded. to request that a conference *is* convened,

■ Local Safeguarding Children's Boards (LSCBs) should have in place for use in the last resort, a quick and straightforward means of resolving differences of opinion

If Concerns are Not Substantiated

■ Social workers and their manager should:

  • Discuss the case with the child, parents and other professionals
  • Decide whether to complete the assessment to determine whether support services may be helpful
  • Consider whether the child's health and development should be re-assessed regularly against specific objectives and who has responsibility for doing this

■ All involved professionals should:

  • Participate in further discussions as necessary

- Contribute to completion of assessment as appropriate
- Provide services as specified in the plan for child
- Review the impact of services delivered as agreed in the plan

Concerns are Substantiated & Child Judged to be Suffering, or Likely to Suffer Significant Harm

■ Social workers and their managers should:

- Convene an initial child protection conference; the timing should depend on the urgency of the case and respond to the needs of the child and the nature and severity of the harm they may be facing; an initial child protection conference should take place within 15 working days of a strategy discussion, or the strategy discussion at which s.47 enquiries were initiated if more than one has been held
- Consider whether any professionals with specialist knowledge should be invited to participate
- Ensure that the child and their parents understand the purpose of the conference and who will attend
- Help prepare the child if s/he is attending or making representations through a third party to the conference; give information about advocacy agencies and explain that the family may bring an advocate, friend or supporter

■ All involved professionals should:

- Contribute to the information their agency provides ahead of the conference, setting out the nature of the agency's involvement with the child and family
- Consider, in conjunction with the Police and the appointed conference chairperson, whether the report can and should be shared with the parents and if so when
- Attend the conference and take part in decision making when invited

Initial Child Protection Conference

■ Following s.47 enquiries, an initial child protection
conference brings together family (and the child
when appropriate), with the supporters, advocates
and professionals most involved with the child and
family, to make decisions about the child's future
safety, health and development. If concerns relate to
an unborn child, consideration should be given as to
whether to hold a child protection conference prior to
the child's birth.

Purpose

■ To bring together and analyse, in an inter-agency
setting, all relevant information and plan how best to
safeguard and promote the welfare of the child. It is
the responsibility of the conference to make
recommendations on how agencies work together to
safeguard the child in future.

■ Conference tasks include:

- Appointing a lead statutory body (either
  Children's Social Care or NSPCC) and a lead
  social worker, who should be a qualified,
  experienced social worker and an employee of
  the lead statutory body
- Identifying membership of the core group of
  professionals and family members who will
  develop and implement the child protection plan

- Establishing timescales for meetings of the core group, production of a child protection plan and for child protection review meetings
- Agreeing an outline child protection plan, with clear actions and timescales, including a clear sense of how much improvement is needed, by when, so that success can be judged clearly

Task Allocation

■ The conference chairperson:

- Is accountable to the Director of Children's Services (DCS)
- Should be a professional, independent of operational and/or line management responsibilities for the case
- Should meet the child and parents in advance to ensure they understand the purpose and the process

NB. If possible the same person should chair subsequent child protection review.

■ Social workers with their managers should:

- Convene, attend and present information about the reason for the conference, their understanding of the child's needs, parental capacity and family and environmental context and evidence of how the child has been abused or neglected and its impact on health and development

- Analyse the information to enable informed decisions about what action is necessary to safeguard and promote the welfare of the child who is the subject of the conference
- Share the conference information with the child and family beforehand (when appropriate)
- Prepare a report for the conference on the child and family which sets out and analyses what is known about the child and family and the local authority's recommendation and
- Record conference decisions and recommendations and ensure action follows

■ All involved professionals should work together to safeguard the child from harm in the future, taking timely, effective action according to the plan agreed.

■ LSCBs should monitor the effectiveness of these arrangements.

Child Protection Plan

Purpose of Child Protection Plan

- The aim of the child protection plan is to:

    - Ensure the child is safe from harm and prevent him or her from suffering further harm
    - Promote the child's health and development
    - Support the family and wider family members to safeguard and promote the welfare of their child, provided it is in the best interests of the child

Task Allocation

- Children's Social Care should:

    - Designate a social worker to be the lead professional as they carry statutory responsibility for the child's welfare
    - Consider the evidence and decide what legal action to take if any, where a child has suffered, or is likely to suffer, significant harm; and
    - Define the local protocol for timeliness of circulating plans after the conference

- Social workers with their managers should:

    - Be the lead professional for inter-agency work with the child and family, coordinating the contribution of family members and professionals into putting the child protection plan into effect
    - Develop the outline child protection plan into a more detailed inter-agency plan and circulate to

relevant professionals (and family when appropriate)

- Undertake direct work with the child and family in accordance with the child protection plan, taking into account the child's wishes and feelings and the views of the parents in so far as they are consistent with the child's welfare
- Complete the child's and family's in-depth assessment, securing contributions from core group members and others as necessary
- Explain the plan to the child in a manner which is in accordance with their age and understanding and agree the plan with the child
- Coordinate reviews of progress against the planned outcomes set out in the plan, updating as required; the first review should be held within 3 months of the initial conference and further reviews at intervals of no more than 6 months for as long as the child remains subject of a child protection plan
- Record decisions and actions agreed at core group meetings as well as the written views of those who were not able to attend, and follow up those actions to ensure they take place; the child protection plan should be updated as necessary
- Lead core group activity

■ Core groups should:

- Meet within 10 working days from the initial child protection conference if the child is the subject of a child protection plan

- Develop the outline child protection plan, based on assessment findings, and set out what needs to change, by how much, and by when in order for the child to be safe and have her/his needs met

- Decide what steps need to be taken, and by whom, to complete the in-depth assessment to inform decisions about the child's safety and welfare

- Implement the child protection plan and take joint responsibility for carrying out the agreed tasks, monitoring progress and outcomes, and refining the plan as needed

Child Protection Review Conference

Purpose

■ The purpose is to:

- Review whether the child is continuing to suffer, or is likely to suffer, significant harm, and review developmental progress against child protection plan outcomes
- Consider whether the child protection plan should continue or should be changed

Task Allocation

■ Social workers with their managers should:

- Attend and lead the organisation of the conference
- Determine when the review conference should be held within 3 months of the initial conference and thereafter at maximum intervals of 6 months
- Provide information to enable informed decisions about what action is necessary to safeguard and promote the welfare of the child who is the subject of the child protection plan, and about the effectiveness and impact of action taken so far
- Share the conference information with the child and family beforehand, when appropriate;
- Record conference outcomes
- Decide whether to initiate family court proceedings (all the children in the household

should be considered, even if concerns are only expressed about one child) if the child is considered to be suffering significant harm

- All involved professionals should:

  - Attend, when invited, and provide details of their involvement with the child and family
  - Produce reports for the child protection review; this information will provide an overview of work undertaken by family members and professionals, and evaluate the impact on the child's welfare against the planned outcomes set out in the child protection plan.

Flow chart 5: After initial & review conferences

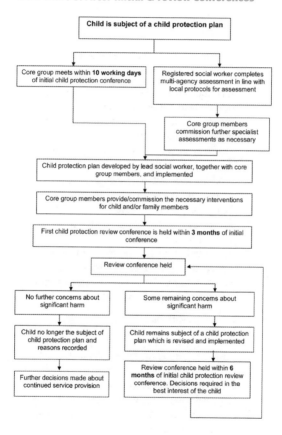

┌───┐
│ **Child is subject of a child protection plan** │
└───┘

┌──────────────────────────────┐   ┌──────────────────────────────┐
│ Core group meets within **10 working days** of initial child protection conference │   │ Registered social worker completes multi-agency assessment in line with local protocols for assessment │
└──────────────────────────────┘   └──────────────────────────────┘

┌──────────────────────────────┐
│ Core group members commission further specialist assessments as necessary │
└──────────────────────────────┘

┌──┐
│ Child protection plan developed by lead social worker, together with core group members, and implemented │
└──┘

┌──┐
│ Core group members provide/commission the necessary interventions for child and/or family members │
└──┘

┌──┐
│ First child protection review conference is held within **3 months** of initial conference │
└──┘

┌──────────────────────────────┐
│ Review conference held │
└──────────────────────────────┘

┌──────────────────────────────┐   ┌──────────────────────────────┐
│ No further concerns about significant harm │   │ Some remaining concerns about significant harm │
└──────────────────────────────┘   └──────────────────────────────┘

┌──────────────────────────────┐   ┌──────────────────────────────┐
│ Child no longer the subject of child protection plan and reasons recorded │   │ Child remains subject of a child protection plan which is revised and implemented │
└──────────────────────────────┘   └──────────────────────────────┘

┌──────────────────────────────┐   ┌──────────────────────────────┐
│ Further decisions made about continued service provision │   │ Review conference held within **6 months** of initial child protection review conference. Decisions required in the best interest of the child │
└──────────────────────────────┘   └──────────────────────────────┘

Discontinuing the Child Protection Plan

■ A child should no longer be the subject of a child protection plan if:

- It is judged that s/he is no longer continuing to, or is likely to, suffer significant harm and therefore no longer requires safeguarding by means of a child protection plan
- The child and family have moved permanently to another local authority area; in such cases, the receiving local authority should convene a child protection conference within 15 working days of being notified of the move and only after this event may the original local authority discontinue its child protection plan or
- The child has reached 18 (to end the plan, the local authority should have a review around the child's birthday planned in advance), has died or has permanently left the United Kingdom.

■ Social workers with their managers should:

- Notify, as a minimum, all agency representatives invited to attend the initial child protection conference that led to the plan
- Consider whether support services are still required and discuss with the child and family what might be needed, based on a re-assessment of the child's needs.

LOCAL SAFEGUARDING CHILDREN BOARDS

Statutory Objectives & Functions

Establishment of a LSCB [s.13 Children Act 2004]

■ S.13 requires each local authority to establish a LSCB for its area and specifies the organisations and individuals (other than the local authority) that should be represented on LSCBs.

Objectives of the LSCB [s.14 Children Act 2004]

■ The objectives of the LSCB are to:

- Coordinate what is done by each person or body represented on the Board for the purposes of safeguarding and promoting the welfare of children in the area
- Ensure the effectiveness of what is done by each such person or body for those purposes

■ Regulation 5 of the Local Safeguarding Children Boards Regulations 2006 sets out that the functions of the LSCB, in relation to the above objectives under s.14 Children Act 2004, are:

- Developing policies and procedures for safeguarding and promoting the welfare of children in the area of the authority, including policies and procedures in relation to (i) the action to be taken where there are concerns about a child's safety or welfare, including thresholds for intervention; (ii) training of persons who work with children or in services affecting the safety and welfare of children; (iii) recruitment and supervision of persons who work with children; (iv) investigation of allegations concerning persons who work with children; (v) safety and welfare of children who are privately fostered; (vi) cooperation with neighbouring children's services authorities and their Board partners

- Communicating to persons and bodies in the area of the authority the need to safeguard and promote the welfare of children, raising their awareness of how this can best be done and encouraging them to do so;

- Monitoring and evaluating the effectiveness of what is done by the authority and their Board partners individually and collectively to safeguard and promote the welfare of children and advising them on ways to improve;

- Participating in the planning of services for children in the area of the authority; and

- Undertaking reviews of serious cases and advising the authority and their Board partners on lessons to be learned.

■ Regulations 5(2) and 6 which relates to the Serious Case Review and Child Death functions are covered on p. 311 and p.318 respectively.

■ Regulation 5(3) provides that a LSCB *may* also engage in any other activity that facilitates, or is conducive to, the achievement of its objectives.

- In order to fulfil its statutory function under reg.5 an LSCB should use data and, as a minimum, should:

  - Assess the effectiveness of the help being provided to children and families, including early help
  - Assess whether LSCB partners are fulfilling their statutory obligations
  - Quality assure practice, including through joint audits of case files involving practitioners and identifying lessons to be learned
  - Monitor and evaluate the effectiveness of training, including multi-agency training, to safeguard and promote the welfare of children; the *Children's Safeguarding Performance Information Framework* at www.education.gov.uk provides a mechanism to help do this by setting out some of the questions a LSCB should consider

- LSCBs do not commission or deliver direct frontline services though they may provide training. While LSCBs do not have the power to direct other organisations they do have a role in making clear where improvement is needed. Each Board partner retains their own existing line of accountability for safeguarding.

Membership of LSCB

- S.13 Children Act 2004 (as amended), sets out that an LSCB must include at least 1 representative of the local authority and each of the other Board partners set out below (although 2 or more Board partners may be represented by the same person).

■ Board partners who must be included in the LSCB are:

- District councils in local government areas which have them
- Chief officer of Police
- Local Probation Trust
- Youth Offending Team
- NHS Commissioning Board and clinical commissioning groups
- NHS Trusts and NHS Foundation Trusts all or most of whose hospitals, establishments and facilities are situated in the local authority area
- Cafcass
- Governor or director of any secure training centre in the area of the authority
- Governor or director of any prison in the area of the authority which ordinarily detains children

■ The Apprenticeships, Skills, Children and Learning Act 2009 amended ss.13 and 14 Children Act 2004 and provided that the local authority must take reasonable steps to ensure that the LSCB includes 2 lay members representing the local community.

■ S.13(4) of the Children Act 2004 (as amended), provides that the local authority must take reasonable steps to ensure the LSCB includes representatives of relevant persons and bodies of such descriptions as may be prescribed. Regulation

3A of the LSCB Regulations prescribes the following persons and bodies:

- Governing body of a maintained school
- Proprietor of a non-maintained special school
- Proprietor of a city technology college, a city college for the technology of the arts or an Academy
- Governing body of a further education institution the main site of which is situated in the authority's area

▪ All schools (including independent schools, Academies and free schools) have duties in relation to safeguarding children and promoting their welfare.

▪ Local authorities should take reasonable steps to ensure that the LSCB includes representatives from of all types of school in their area. A system of representation should be identified to enable all schools to receive information and feed back comments to their representatives on the LSCB.

▪ The LSCB should work with the Local Family Justice Board. They should also work with the health and wellbeing board, informing and drawing on the Joint Strategic Needs Assessment.

▪ In exceptional circumstances an LSCB can cover more than one local authority. Where boundaries between LSCBs and their partner organisations are not coterminous, e.g. with health organisations and Police authorities, LSCBs should collaborate as necessary on establishing common policies and procedures and joint ways of working.

■ Members of an LSCB should be people with a strategic role in relation to safeguarding and promoting the welfare of children within their organisation. They should be able to:

- Speak for their organisation with authority
- Commit their organisation on policy and practice matters
- Hold their own organisation to account and hold others to account

■ The LSCB should either include on its Board, or be able to draw on appropriate expertise and advice from, frontline professionals from all the relevant sectors, including a designated doctor and nurse, the Director of Public Health, Principal Child and Family Social Worker and the voluntary and community sector.

■ Lay members will operate as full members of the LSCB, participating as appropriate on the Board itself and on relevant committees. Lay members should help to make links between the LSCB and community groups, support stronger public engagement in local child safety issues and an improved public understanding of the LSCB's child protection work. A local authority may pay lay members.

■ The Lead Member for Children should be a participating observer of the LSCB. In practice this means routinely attending meetings as an observer and receiving all its written reports

Chairperson, Accountability & Resourcing

■ In order to provide effective scrutiny, the LSCB should be independent. It should not be subordinate to, nor subsumed within, other local structures.

■ Every LSCB should have an independent chairperson who can hold all agencies to account.

■ It is the responsibility of the Chief Executive (Head of Paid Service) to appoint or remove the LSCB chairperson with the agreement of a panel including LSCB partners and lay members. The Chief Executive, drawing on other LSCB partners and, when appropriate, the Lead Member will hold the chairperson to account for the effective working of the LSCB.

■ The LSCB chairperson should work closely with all LSCB partners and particularly with the Director of Children's Services (DCS). The DCS has the responsibility within the local authority, under s.18 Children Act 2004, for improving outcomes for children, local authority Children's Social Care functions and local cooperation arrangements for children's services. See Department for Education statutory guidance on *The roles and responsibilities of the Director of Children's Services and Lead Member for Children's Services* at www.education.gov. uk which expands on this role.

- The chairperson must publish an annual report on the effectiveness of safeguarding and promoting the welfare of children in the area (a statutory requirement of s.14A Children Act 2004). The report should be published in relation to the preceding financial year and fit with local agencies' planning, commissioning and budget cycles. It should be submitted to the Chief Executive, Leader of the Council, local Police and Crime Commissioner and chairperson of the Health and Wellbeing board.

- The report should provide a rigorous and transparent assessment of the performance and effectiveness of local services. It should identify areas of weakness, the causes of those weaknesses and the action being taken to address them as well as other proposals for action. The report should include lessons from reviews undertaken within the reporting period.

- The report should also list the contributions made to the LSCB by partner agencies and details of what the LSCB has spent, including on Child Death Reviews, SCRs and other specific expenditure such as learning or training events. All member organisations have an obligation to provide the LSCB with reliable resources (including finance) that enable it to be strong and effective. Members should share the financial responsibility for the LSCB in such a way that a disproportionate burden does not fall on a small number of partner agencies.

- All chairpersons should have access to training and development opportunities, including peer networking. They should also have an LSCB business manager and other discrete support as is necessary for them, and the LSCB, to perform effectively.

Information Sharing

- Every LSCB should play a strong role in supporting information sharing between and within organisations and addressing any barriers to information sharing. This should include ensuring that a culture of information sharing is developed and supported as necessary by multi-agency training.

- In addition, the LSCB can require a person or body to comply with a request for information (s.14A Children Act 2004 inserted by s.8 Children, Schools and Families Act 2010.). This can only take place where the information is essential to carrying out LSCB statutory functions.

- Any request for information about individuals must be 'necessary' and 'proportionate' to the reasons for the request. LSCBs should be mindful of the burden of requests and should explain why the information is needed.

Learning & Improvement Framework

■ Professionals and organisations protecting children need to reflect on the quality of their services and learn from their own practice and that of others. Good practice should be shared so that there is a growing understanding of what works well. Conversely, when things go wrong there needs to be a rigorous, objective analysis of what happened and why, so that important lessons can be learnt and services improved to reduce the risk of future harm to children.

■ These processes should be transparent, with findings of reviews shared publicly. The findings are not only important for the professionals involved locally in cases. Everyone across the country has an interest in understanding both what works well and also why things can go wrong.

■ LSCBs should maintain a local learning and improvement framework which is shared across local organisations who work with children and families. This framework should enable organisations to be clear about their responsibilities, to learn from experience and improve services as a result.

■ Each local framework should support the work of the LSCB and their partners so that:

•   Reviews are conducted regularly, not only on cases which meet statutory criteria, but also on other cases which can provide useful insights into

the way organisations are working together to
safeguard and protect the welfare of children

- Reviews look at what happened in a case, and
  why, and what action will be taken to learn from
  the review findings
- Action results in lasting improvements which
  safeguard and promote the welfare of children
  and help protect them from harm
- There is transparency about the issues arising
  from individual cases and the actions which
  organisations are taking in response to them,
  including sharing the final reports of SCRs with
  the public

▨ The local framework should cover the full range of
reviews and audits which are aimed at driving
improvements to safeguard and promote the welfare
of children. Some of these reviews i.e. SCRs and child
death reviews are required under legislation. It is
important that LSCBs understand the criteria for
determining whether a statutory review is required
and always conduct those reviews when necessary.

▨ LSCBs should also conduct reviews of cases which do
not meet the criteria for an SCR, but which can
provide valuable lessons about how organisations are
working together to safeguard and promote the
welfare of children. Although not required by statute
these reviews are important for highlighting good
practice and identifying improvements to be made to
local services. Such reviews may be conducted either
by a single organisation or by a number working

together. LSCBs should follow the principles in *Working Together to Safeguard Children* 2013 when conducting them.

▪ Reviews are not ends in themselves. The purpose of these reviews is to identify improvements which are needed and to consolidate good practice. LSCBs and their partner organisations should translate the findings from reviews into programmes of action which lead to sustainable improvements and the prevention of death, serious injury or harm to children.

▪ The different types of review include:

- Serious Case Review: for every case where abuse or neglect is known or suspected and *either* a child dies or is seriously harmed and there are concerns about how organisations or professionals worked together to safeguard the child
- Child death review (a review of all child deaths up to the age of 18)
- A review of a child protection incident which falls below the threshold for a SCR
- A review or audit of practice in one or more agencies

Principles for Learning & Improvement

▪ The following principles should be applied by LSCBs and their partner organisations to all reviews:

- There should be a culture of continuous learning and improvement across the organisations that work together to safeguard and promote the welfare of children, identifying opportunities to draw on what works and promote good practice
- The approach taken to reviews should be proportionate according to the scale and level of complexity of the issues being examined
- Reviews of serious cases should be led by individuals who are independent of the case under review and of the organisations whose actions are being reviewed
- Professionals must be involved fully in reviews and invited to contribute their perspectives without fear of being blamed for actions they took in good faith
- Families, including surviving children, should be invited to contribute to reviews; they should understand how they are going to be involved and their expectations should be managed appropriately and sensitively; this is important for ensuring that the child is at the centre of the process see *Family involvement in case reviews*, (British Association for the Study and Prevention of Child Abuse and Neglect BASPCAN) at www.baspcan.org.uk
- Final reports of SCRs *must be published*, including the LSCB's response to the review findings, in order to achieve transparency; the impact of SCRs and other reviews on improving services to children and families and on reducing

the incidence of deaths or serious harm to children must also be described in LSCB annual reports and will inform inspections

- Improvement must be sustained through regular monitoring and follow up so that the findings from these reviews make a real impact on improving outcomes for children

◼ SCRs and other case reviews should be conducted in a way which:

- Recognises the complex circumstances in which professionals work together to safeguard children
- Seeks to understand precisely who did what and the underlying reasons that led individuals and organisations to act as they did
- Seeks to understand practice from the viewpoint of the individuals and organisations involved at the time rather than using hindsight
- Is transparent about the way data is collected and analysed
- Makes use of relevant research and case evidence to inform the findings

◼ LSCBs may use any learning model which is consistent with the principles in *Working Together to Safeguard Children* 2013, including the systems methodology recommended by Professor Munro, see *The Munro Review of Child Protection: Final Report: A Child Centred System*, Cm 8062, May 2011 at www.education.gov.uk

Serious Case Reviews

- Regulation 5 of the Safeguarding Children Boards Regulations 2006 sets out the functions of LSCBs. This includes the requirement for them to undertake reviews of serious cases in specified circumstances. Regulation 5(1) (e) and (2) set out an LSCB's function in relation to serious case reviews, namely:

  - Undertaking reviews of 'serious cases' and advising the authority and their Board partners on lessons to be learned [reg.5(1)(e)]

- A 'serious case' is one where:

  - Abuse or neglect of a child is known or suspected [reg.5(2)(a); and
  - Either (i) the child has died or (ii) s/he has been seriously harmed, and there is cause for concern as to the way in which the authority, their Board partners or other relevant persons have worked together to safeguard the child [reg 5(2)(b)]

- Cases which meet one of these criteria i.e. reg.5(2)(a) and (b)(i) or reg.5(2)(a) and (b)(ii) must always trigger an SCR. In addition, an SCR should always be carried out when a child dies in custody, in Police custody, on remand or following sentencing, in a Young Offender Institution, in a secure training centre or a secure children's home, or where the child was detained under the Mental Health Act 2005. Regulation 5(2)(b)(i) includes cases where a child died by suspected suicide.

■ When a case is being considered under regulation 5(2)(b)(ii), unless it is clear that there are no concerns about inter-agency working, the LSCB must commission an SCR.

■ The final decision on whether to conduct the SCR rests with the LSCB chairperson. If an SCR is not required because the criteria in regulation 5(2) are not met, the LSCB may still decide to commission an SCR or they may choose to commission an alternative form of case review.

■ LSCBs should consider conducting reviews on cases which do not meet the SCR criteria. They will also want to review instances of good practice and consider how these can be shared and embedded. LSCBs are free to decide how best to conduct these reviews. The LSCB should oversee implementation of actions resulting from these reviews and reflect on progress in its annual report.

National Panel of Independent Experts on SCRs

■ A national panel of independent experts advises LSCBs about the initiation and publication of SCRs. The role of the panel will be to support LSCBs in ensuring that appropriate action is taken to learn from serious incidents in all cases where the statutory SCR criteria are met and to ensure that those lessons are shared through publication of final SCR reports. The panel will also report to the government their views of how the SCR system is working.

▣ The panel's remit will include advising LSCBs about:

- Application of the SCR criteria
- Appointment of reviewers
- Publication of SCR reports

▣ LSCBs should have regard to the panel's advice when deciding whether or not to initiate an SCR, when appointing reviewers and when considering publication of SCR reports. LSCB Chairs and LSCB members should comply with requests from the panel as far as possible, including requests for information such as copies of SCR reports and invitations to attend meetings.

▣ In doing so LSCBs will be exercising their powers under Regulation 5(3) of the Local Safeguarding Children Board Regulations 2006 which states that 'an LSCB may also engage in any other activity that facilitates, or is conducive to, the achievement of its objective'.

SCR Checklist

▣ *Decisions whether to initiate an SCR*: The LSCB for the area in which the child is normally resident should decide whether an incident notified to it meets the criteria for an SCR. This decision should normally be made within 1 month of notification of the incident. The final decision rests with the chairperson of the LSCB. The chairperson may seek peer challenge from another LSCB chairperson when considering this decision and also at other stages in the SCR process.

■ The LSCB must let Ofsted and the national panel of independent experts know its decision.

■ If the LSCB decides *not* to initiate an SCR, the decision may be subject to scrutiny by the national panel. The LSCB should provide information to the panel on request to inform its deliberations and the LSCB chairperson should be prepared to attend in person to give evidence to the panel.

■ *Appointing reviewers*: The LSCB must appoint one or more suitable individuals to lead the SCR who have demonstrated that they are qualified to conduct reviews using the approach set out in this guidance. The lead reviewer should be independent of the LSCB and the organisations involved in the case. The LSCB should provide the national panel of independent experts with the name/s of the individual/s they appoint to conduct the SCR. The LSCB should consider carefully any advice from the independent expert panel about appointment of reviewers.

■ *Engagement of organisations*: The LSCB should ensure that there is appropriate representation in the review process of professionals and organisations who were involved with the child and family. The priority should be to engage organisations in a way which will ensure that important factors in the case can be identified and appropriate action taken to make improvements. The LSCB may decide as part of the SCR to ask each relevant organisation to provide information in writing about its involvement with the child who is the subject of the review.

■ *Timescale for SCR completion*: The LSCB should aim for completion of an SCR within 6 months of initiating it. If this is not possible (for example, because of potential prejudice to related court proceedings), every effort should be made while the SCR is in progress to capture points from the case about improvements needed and take corrective action.

■ *Agreeing improvement action*: The LSCB should oversee the process of agreeing with partners what action they need to take in light of the SCR findings.

■ *Publication of reports*: All reviews of cases meeting the SCR criteria should result in a report which is published and readily accessible on the LSCB's website for a minimum of 12 months. Thereafter the report should be made available on request. This is important to support national sharing of lessons learnt and good practice in writing and publishing SCRs. From the very start of the SCR the fact that the report will be published should be taken into consideration. SCR reports should be written in such a way that publication will not be likely to harm the welfare of any children or vulnerable adults involved in the case.

■ Final SCR reports should:

- Provide a sound analysis of what happened in the case, and why, and what needs to happen in order to reduce the risk of recurrence
- Be written in plain English and in a way that can be easily understood by professionals and the public alike
- Be suitable for publication without needing to be amended or redacted

▪ LSCBs should publish, either as part of the SCR report or in a separate document, information about actions which have already been taken in response to the review findings, the impact these actions have had on improving services and what more will be done.

▪ When compiling and preparing to publish reports, LSCBs should consider carefully how best to manage the impact of publication on children, family members and others affected by the case. LSCBs must comply with the Data Protection Act 1998 in relation to SCRs, including when compiling or publishing the report, and must comply also with any other restrictions on publication of information, such as court orders.

▪ LSCBs should send copies of all SCR reports to the national panel of independent experts at least one week before publication. If an LSCB considers that a SCR report should *not* be published, it should inform the panel which will provide advice to the LSCB. The LSCB should provide all relevant information to the panel on request, to inform its deliberations.

Child Death Reviews

- The LSCB functions in relation to child deaths are set out in Regulation 6 of the Local Safeguarding Children Boards Regulations 2006, made under s.14(2) Children Act 2004. The LSCB is responsible for:

- Collecting and analysing information about each death with a view to identifying (i) any case giving rise to the need for a review mentioned in regulation 5(1)(e) i.e. a SCR; (ii) any matters of concern affecting the safety and welfare of children in the area of the authority; (iii) any wider public health or safety concerns arising from a particular death or from a pattern of deaths in that area [reg.6(a)]

- (b) Putting in place procedures for ensuring that there is a coordinated response by the authority, their Board partners and other relevant persons to an unexpected death [reg.6(b)]

- Each death of a child is a tragedy and enquiries should keep an appropriate balance between forensic and medical requirements and supporting the family at a difficult time. Professionals supporting parents and family members should assure them that the objective of the child death review process is not to allocate blame, but to learn lessons. The Review will help to prevent further such child deaths. See the explanatory leaflet 'Child death review: a guide for parents and carers' produced by the Foundation for

Sudden Infant death (FSID) and available from www. education.gov.uk

■ Responsibility for determining cause of death rests with the Coroner or doctor who signs the medical certificate of the cause of death (and is not the responsibility of the Child Death Overview Panel (CDOP)).

Responsibilities of LSCB for Child Death Reviews

■ The LSCB is responsible for ensuring that a review of each death of a child normally resident in the LSCB's area is undertaken by a Child Death Overview Panel (CDOP). The Panel will have a fixed core membership drawn from organisations represented on the LSCB with flexibility to co-opt other relevant professionals to discuss certain types of death as/when appropriate. The Panel should include a professional from public health as well as child health. It should be chaired by the LSCB chairperson's representative. That individual should not be involved directly in providing services to children and families in the area. One or more LSCBs can choose to share a CDOP. CDOPs responsible for reviewing deaths from larger populations are better able to identify significant recurrent contributory factors.

■ LSCBs should be informed of the deaths of all children normally resident in their geographical area. The LSCB chairperson should decide who will be the designated person to whom the death notification and other data on each death should be sent (the

DfE has a list of people designated by the CDOP to receive notifications of child death information).

■ LSCBs should use sources available, such as professional contacts or the Media, to find out about cases when a child normally resident in their area dies abroad. The LSCB should inform the CDOP of such cases so that the deaths of these children can be reviewed.

■ In cases where organisations in more than one LSCB area have known about or have had contact with the child, lead responsibility should sit with the LSCB for the area in which the child was normally resident at the time of death. Other LSCBs or local organisations which have had involvement in the case should cooperate in jointly planning and undertaking the child death review. In the case of a looked after child, the LSCB for the area of the local authority looking after the child should exercise lead responsibility for conducting the child death review, involving other LSCBs with an interest or whose lead agencies have had involvement as appropriate.

Specific Responsibilities of Relevant Bodies in Relation to Child Deaths

■ *Registrars of Births and Deaths* (Children & Young Persons Act 2008): Have a requirement to:

• Supply the LSCB with information which they have about the death of persons under 18 they have registered or re-registered

- Notify LSCBs if they issue a 'Certificate of No Liability to Register' where it appears that the deceased was or may have been under the age of 18 at the time of death.
- Send the information to the appropriate LSCB (the one which covers the sub-district in which the register is kept) no later than 7 days from the date of registration

- *Coroners* (Coroners Rules 1984 (as amended by the Coroners (Amendment) Rules 2008) have a:

  - Duty to inquire and may require evidence
  - Duty to inform the LSCB for the area in which the child died within 3 working days of the fact of an inquest or post mortem
  - Power to share information with LSCBs for the purposes of carrying out their functions, including reviewing child deaths and undertaking SCRs

- *The Registrar General* (s.32 Children and Young Persons Act 2008) has a power to share child death information with the Secretary of State, including about children who die abroad.

- *Medical Examiners* (Coroners and Justice Act 2009). It is anticipated that from 2014 Medical Examiners will be required to share information with LSCBs about child deaths that are not investigated by a Coroner.

- *Clinical Commissioning Groups* (Health and Social Care Act 2012): Employ, or have arrangements in place to secure the expertise of, consultant paediatricians whose designated responsibilities are to provide advice on:

- Commissioning paediatric services from paediatricians with expertise in undertaking enquiries into unexpected deaths in childhood, and from medical investigative services
- The organisation of such services

■ A summary of the child death processes to be followed when reviewing all child deaths and the processes for undertaking a rapid response when a child dies unexpectedly, are set out in flowcharts 6 and 7 respectively.

■ Every LSCB is required to supply anonymised information on child deaths to the DfE. This is so that it can commission research and publish nationally comparable analyses of these deaths. '*Detailed guidance on how to supply the information on child deaths*' is available from www.education.gov.uk

Specific Responsibilities of Relevant Professionals When Responding to the Unexpected Death of a Child

■ *The designated paediatrician for unexpected deaths in childhood*: Should ensure that relevant professionals i.e. Coroner, Police and Children's Social Care are informed of the death; coordinate the team of professionals (involved before and/or after the death) which is convened when a child who dies unexpectedly (accessing professionals from specialist agencies as necessary to support the core team).

■ S/he should also convene multi-agency discussions after the initial and final initial post mortem results are available.

Responsibilities of Child Death Overview Panel (CDOP)

■ The functions of the CDOP include:

- Reviewing all child deaths up to the age of 18, excluding stillborn babies and planned terminations carried out within the law

- Collecting and collating information on each child and seeking relevant information from professionals and, when appropriate, family

- Discussing each child's case, and providing relevant information or any specific actions related to individual families to those professionals who are involved directly with the family so that they, in turn, can convey this information in a sensitive manner to the family

- Determining whether the death was deemed 'preventable' i.e. those deaths in which modifiable factors may have contributed to the death and decide what, if any, actions could be taken to prevent future such deaths

- Making recommendations to the LSCB or other relevant bodies promptly so that action can be taken to prevent future such deaths if possible

- Identifying patterns or trends in local data and reporting these to the LSCB
- When a suspicion arises that neglect or abuse may have been a factor in the child's death, referring a case back to the LSCB chairperson for consideration of whether an SCR is required
- Agreeing local procedures for responding to unexpected deaths of children
- Cooperating with regional and national initiatives e.g. the National Clinical Outcome Review Programme – to identify lessons on the prevention of child deaths

■ The aggregated findings from all child deaths should inform local strategic planning, including the local Joint Strategic Needs Assessment, on how to best safeguard and promote the welfare of children in the area. Each CDOP should prepare an annual report of relevant information for the LSCB. This information should in turn inform the LSCB annual report.

Definition of Preventable Child Death

■ For the purpose of producing aggregate national data, *Working Together to Safeguard Children* 2013 defines 'preventable' child deaths as those in which modifiable factors may have contributed to the death. These factors are defined as those which, by means of nationally or locally achievable interventions, could be modified to reduce the risk of future child deaths.

■ In reviewing the death of each child, the CDOP should consider modifiable factors, for example in the family and environment, parenting capacity or service provision, and consider what action could be taken locally and what action could be taken at a regional or national level.

Action by Professionals When a Child Dies Unexpectedly

Definition of an Unexpected Death of a Child

■ *Working Together to Safeguard Children* 2013 defines an 'unexpected' death as the death of an infant or child (less than 18 years old) which was not anticipated as a significant possibility for example, 24 hours before the death; or where there was a similarly unexpected collapse or incident leading to or precipitating the events which lead to the death.

■ The designated paediatrician responsible for unexpected deaths in childhood should be consulted when professionals are uncertain about whether the death is unexpected. If in doubt, the processes for unexpected child deaths should be followed until the available evidence enables a different decision to be made.

■ As set out the Local Safeguarding Children Boards Regulations 2006, LSCBs are responsible for putting in place procedures for ensuring that there is a coordinated response by the authority, their Board partners and other relevant persons to an unexpected death.

■ When a child dies suddenly and unexpectedly, the consultant clinician (in a hospital setting) or the professional confirming the fact of death (if the child is not taken immediately to an A&E department) should inform the local designated paediatrician with responsibility for unexpected child deaths at the same time as informing the Coroner and Police. Police will begin an investigation into the sudden or unexpected death on behalf of the Coroner. A paediatrician should initiate an immediate information sharing and planning discussion between lead agencies i.e. Health, Police and Children's Social Care to decide what should happen next and who will do it.

- Joint responsibilities of the professionals involved with the child include:

  - Responding quickly to the child's death in accordance with the locally agreed procedures
  - Maintaining a rapid response protocol with all agencies, consistent with the Kennedy principles and current investigative practice from the Association of Chief Police Officers
  - Making immediate enquiries into and evaluating the reasons for and circumstances of the death, in agreement with the Coroner
  - Liaising with the Coroner and the pathologist
  - Undertaking the types of enquiries/ investigations that relate to the current responsibilities of their respective organisations
  - Collecting information about the death
  - Providing support to the bereaved family, referring to specialist bereavement services where necessary and keeping them up to date with information about the child's death; and

- Gaining consent early from the family for the examination of their medical notes

■ If the child dies suddenly or unexpectedly at home or in the community, the child should normally be taken to an Emergency Department rather than a mortuary. In some cases when a child dies at home or in the community, Police may decide that it is not appropriate to immediately move the child's body, for example because forensic examinations are needed.

■ As soon as possible after arrival at a hospital, the child should be examined by a consultant paediatrician and a detailed history taken from the parents or carers. The purpose of obtaining this information is to understand the cause of death and identify anything suspicious about it. In all cases when a child dies in hospital, or is taken to hospital after dying, the hospital should allocate a member of staff to remain with the parents and support them through the process.

■ If the child has died at home or in the community, the lead Police investigator and senior health care professional should decide whether there should be a visit to the place where the child died, how soon (ideally within 24 hours) and who should attend. This should almost always take place for cases of sudden infant death.

■ After this visit the senior investigator, visiting health care professional, GP, health visitor or school nurse and Children's Social Care representative should consider whether there is any information to raise concerns that neglect or abuse contributed to the child's death.

- When a child dies unexpectedly, all registered providers of healthcare services must notify the Care Quality Commission of the death of a service user – *but NHS providers may discharge this duty by notifying the National Health Service Commissioning Board* (Regulation 16 of the Care Quality Commission (Registration) Regulations 2009).

- If a young person dies at work, the Health and Safety Executive should be informed. Youth Offending Teams' reviews of safeguarding and public protection incidents (including the deaths of children under their supervision) should also feed into the CDOP child death processes.

- If there is a criminal investigation, the team of professionals must consult the lead Police investigator and the Crown Prosecution Service to ensure that their enquiries do not prejudice any criminal proceedings. If the child dies in custody, there will be an investigation by the Prisons and Probation Ombudsman (or by the Independent Police Complaints Commission in the case of Police custody). Organisations who worked with the child will be required to cooperate with that investigation.

Involvement of Coroner & Pathologist

■ If a doctor is not able to issue a medical certificate of the cause of death, the lead professional or investigator must report the child's death to the Coroner in accordance with a protocol agreed with the local coronial service. The Coroner must investigate violent or unnatural death, or death of no known cause, and all deaths where a person is in custody at the time of death. The Coroner will then have jurisdiction over the child's body at all times. Unless the death is natural a public inquest will be held. See Ministry of Justice *Guidance for Coroners and Local Safeguarding Children Boards on the supply of information concerning the death of children at www.justice.gov.uk*

■ The Coroner will order a post mortem examination to be carried out as soon as possible by the most appropriate pathologist available (this may be a paediatric pathologist, forensic pathologist or both) who will perform the examination according to guidelines and protocols laid down by the Royal College of Pathologists. The designated paediatrician will collate and share information about the circumstances of the child's death with the pathologist in order to inform this process.

■ If the death is unnatural or the cause of death cannot be confirmed, the coroner will hold an inquest. Professionals and organisations who are involved in the child death review process must cooperate with the Coroner and provide her/him with a joint report about the circumstances of the child's death. This report should include a review of all medical, Children's Social Care and educational records on the child. The report should be delivered to the Coroner within 28 days of the death unless crucial information is not yet available.

Action After the Post Mortem

- Although the results of the post mortem belong to the Coroner, it should be possible for the paediatrician, pathologist, and the lead Police investigator to discuss findings as soon as possible, and the Coroner should be informed immediately of initial results. If these results suggest evidence of abuse or neglect as a possible cause of death, the paediatrician should inform the Police and Children's Social Care immediately. S/he should also inform the LSCB chairperson so s/he can consider whether the criteria are met for initiating an SCR.

- Shortly after the initial post mortem results become available, the designated paediatrician for unexpected child deaths should convene a multi-agency case discussion, including all those who knew the family and were involved in investigating the child's death.

- The professionals should review any further available information, including any that may raise concerns about safeguarding issues. A further multi-agency case discussion should be convened by the designated paediatrician, or a paediatrician acting as their deputy, as soon as the final post mortem result is available. This is in order to share information about the cause of death or factors that may have contributed to the death and to plan future care of the family.

■ The designated paediatrician should arrange for a record of the discussion to be sent to the coroner, to inform the inquest and cause of death, and to the relevant CDOP, to inform the child death review. At the case discussion, it should be agreed how detailed information about the cause of the child's death will be shared, and by whom, with the parents, and who will offer the parents on-going support.

Flowchart 6: Process to be followed for all child deaths

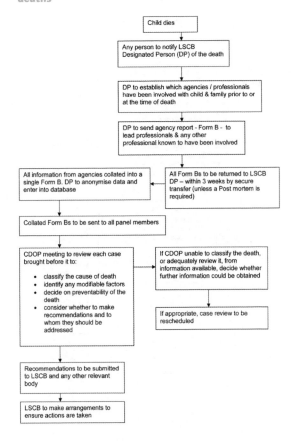

Child dies

↓

Any person to notify LSCB Designated Person (DP) of the death

↓

DP to establish which agencies / professionals have been involved with child & family prior to or at the time of death

↓

DP to send agency report - Form B - to lead professionals & any other professional known to have been involved

↓

All Form Bs to be returned to LSCB DP – within 3 weeks by secure transfer (unless a Post mortem is required)

↓

All information from agencies collated into a single Form B. DP to anonymise data and enter into database

↓

Collated Form Bs to be sent to all panel members

↓

CDOP meeting to review each case brought before it to:

- classify the cause of death
- identify any modifiable factors
- decide on preventability of the death
- consider whether to make recommendations and to whom they should be addressed

→

If CDOP unable to classify the death, or adequately review it, from information available, decide whether further information could be obtained

↓

If appropriate, case review to be rescheduled

↓

Recommendations to be submitted to LSCB and any other relevant body

↓

LSCB to make arrangements to ensure actions are taken

Flowchart 7: Process for rapid response to unexpected death of a child

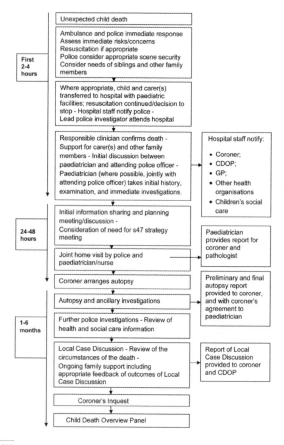

First 2–4 hours

Unexpected child death

Ambulance and police immediate response
Assess immediate risks/concerns
Resuscitation if appropriate
Police consider appropriate scene security
Consider needs of siblings and other family members

Where appropriate, child and carer(s) transferred to hospital with paediatric facilities; resuscitation continued/decision to stop - Hospital staff notify police - Lead police investigator attends hospital

Responsible clinician confirms death - Support for carer(s) and other family members - Initial discussion between paediatrician and attending police officer - Paediatrician (where possible, jointly with attending police officer) takes initial history, examination, and immediate investigations.

Hospital staff notify:

- Coroner;
- CDOP;
- GP;
- Other health organisations
- Children's social care

24–48 hours

Initial information sharing and planning meeting/discussion - Consideration of need for s47 strategy meeting

Joint home visit by police and paediatrician/nurse

Paediatrician provides report for coroner and pathologist

Coroner arranges autopsy

Autopsy and ancillary investigations

Preliminary and final autopsy report provided to coroner, and with coroner's agreement to paediatrician

1–6 months

Further police investigations - Review of health and social care information

Local Case Discussion - Review of the circumstances of the death - Ongoing family support including appropriate feedback of outcomes of Local Case Discussion

Report of Local Case Discussion provided to coroner and CDOP

Coroner's Inquest

Child Death Overview Panel

LAW RELEVANT TO CHILD PROTECTION

Primary Legislation

■ The main sources of English primary legislation relating to the safeguarding and protection of children are:

- Children Act 1989
- Provisions of Criminal Justice Act 1991 (as amended) relating to use of video recording in criminal proceedings
- Part IV Family Law Act 1996
- Protection of Children Act 1999
- Protection From Harassment Act 1997
- Education Act 2002
- Sexual Offences Act 2003
- Children Act 2004
- Safeguarding Vulnerable Groups Act 2006
- Children and Young Persons Act 2008

■ In discharging any of their responsibilities, including child protection s.6 HRA 1998 requires all 'public authorities' e.g. Children's Social Care, Health Trusts, Police, courts etc, to act toward children and adults in ways which are compatible with the European Convention on Human Rights with respect to:

- Article 2 Respect to Life
- Article 3 Prohibition of Torture
- Article 4 Prohibition of Slavery and Forced Labour
- Article 5 Right to Liberty and Security
- Article 6 Right to a Fair Trial

- Article 7 No Punishment Without Law
- Article 8 Right to Respect for Private and Family Life
- Article 9 Freedom of Thought, Conscience and Religion
- Article 10 Freedom of Expression
- Article 11 Freedom of Assembly and Association
- Article 12 Right to Marry

■ Article 14 of the Convention provides that the enjoyment of the above rights must be allowed without discrimination on any ground such as sex, race, colour, language, religion, political or other opinion, national or social origin, association with a national minority, property, birth or other status.

■ A key concept of the Convention of particular relevance to child protection work is that of 'proportionality' i.e. any interference with a person's rights must be sanctioned by law, go no further than necessary and be proportionate to meet a 'pressing social need'.

■ For example, with respect to Article 8 – Respect for Private and Family Life, public authorities can override the right if it is necessary for 'public safety, to prevent crime, to protect health or morals or for the protection of the rights and freedoms of others'.

Inter-agency Co-operation [s.27 Children Act 1989]

■ There is a mutual obligation on local authorities to assist one another unless this is in conflict with their own statutory duties.

Co-operation to Improve Well-being [s.10 Children Act 2004]

- Each CSA must make arrangements to promote co-operation between:

  - The authority
  - Each of the authority's relevant partners and
  - Such other persons or bodies as it considers appropriate engaged in activities in relation to children in the authority's area

Arrangements to Safeguard & Promote Welfare [s.11 Children Act 2004]

- Arrangements are to be made with a view to improving well-being of children in the area so far as relating to:

  - Physical and mental health
  - Protection from harm and neglect
  - Education, training and recreation
  - The contribution made by them to society
  - Emotional, social and economic well-being

- The relevant partners of a CSA in must co-operate with the authority in the making of such arrangements.

- S.11 applies to each of the following:

  - Local authorities and district councils that provide children's services, which includes children's and adult social care services, early years and childcare, education services, public health, housing, sport, culture and leisure services, licensing authorities, youth services
  - NHS organisations – the NHS Commissioning Board and clinical commissioning groups, NHS Trusts and NHS Foundation Trusts
  - Police, including police and crime commissioners and the chief officer of each police force in

England (and the Mayor's Office for Policing and Crime in London)
- British Transport Police
- Probation Service
- Governors/Directors of Prisons and Young Offender Institutions
- Directors of Secure Training Centres and
- Youth Offending Teams/Services

Prevention of Neglect & Abuse
[Sch.2 Para.4 Children Act 1989]

- Each local authority must take reasonable steps through provision of family support services to prevent children within its area suffering ill treatment or neglect.

- The local authority must inform any other local authority if a child likely to suffer harm lives, or proposes to live in its area.

Local Authority Duty to Make Enquiries [s.47(1)(a)(i)–(iii) as amended by Crime & Disorder Act 1998] Children Act 1989]

- When told a child is subject of an Emergency Protection Order, Police Powers of Protection (see below), or the local authority has reasonable cause to suspect s/he is suffering/likely to suffer 'significant harm', or has contravened a ban imposed under the Crime and Disorder Act 1998, it must make enquiries to enable a decision on any necessary action to safeguard and promote the child's welfare.

  NB. The fact it need only be reasonable cause to suspect rather than believe was emphasised in R (On the Application of S) v Swindon BC & Another [2001] 3 FCR 702. Curfew contravention enquiries must be begun as soon as practicable and in any case within 48 hours of receiving information [s.47 (1)(a)(iii) CA 1989 inserted by s.15(4) CDA 1998

- It is the duty of any local authority, education, housing or health trust, and the NSPCC (unless unreasonable to do so) to assist these enquiries e.g. provision of relevant information and advice [s.47 (9); (11) CA 1989].

  NB. S.53 CA 2004 amended s.47 CA 1989 so that there now exists an obligation on the local authority to seek the wishes and feelings of the child and (having regard to age and understanding) give them due consideration when undertaking enquiries

■ In Z v the UK [2001] 2 FLR 612(Formerly X v Bedfordshire CC) (HL), the European Court, ruled that failure by Bedfordshire County Council over 4 years to respond appropriately to concerns about 4 children who were victims of abuse and neglect by their parents, disclosed a breach of their human rights under Articles 3 (Freedom From Degrading Or Inhuman Treatment), and Article 13 (No Access To An Effective Remedy).

Provision of Accommodation to Protect Child [Sch.2 Para.5 Children Act 1989]

■ If it appears to a local authority that a child living on particular premises is suffering or is likely to suffer ill treatment at the hands of another person living there, and that other person proposes to move out, the local authority may assist her/him to obtain alternative accommodation.

Emergency Protection Order (EPO) [s.44 Children Act 1989]

Applications

■ By anyone without notice to the other parties, to a court or an individual magistrate.

NB. It has been argued in Scotland that such applications being made without notice are in breach of Article 6 (Right To a Fair Trial). Reference might also be made the 'proportionality principle' [see above].

Grounds

■ A court must be satisfied that:

- There is reasonable cause to believe child is likely to suffer 'significant harm' if not removed to accommodation provided by the applicant or does not remain in current location e.g. hospital [s.44 (1) (a) CA 1989] or
- The local authority or NSPCC enquiry is at risk of being frustrated by unreasonable refusal of access [s.44 (1) (b) or (c) respectively

NB. The social worker or NSPCC officer must produce identification. Early morning removal of a child is only justified if clear grounds exist that significant harm would otherwise occur or where vital evidence is obtainable only by such means [Re A (Minors) [1992] 1 All ER 153] and is proportionate to the end sought to be achieved (i.e. protection of the health of children – Articles 8(1) & (2) of the Convention). For the meaning of 'reasonable cause to suspect' here and in s. 47, see R on the app of S v Swindon Borough Council [2001] 3 FCR 702.

Effect

- Gives applicant parental responsibility and right to remove/prevent removal of child.

- If, during the course of an EPO, it appears to the applicant that it would be safe to return the child/ allow her/him to leave the place in which s/he has been detained, the applicant must do this.

- If the child is returned home and it proves necessary (within the time limit of the EPO) the order can be reactivated.

Duration

- Up to 8 days with 1 possible extension up to a further 7 days.

- If the last day of an 8 day order falls on a public holiday (Christmas, Good Friday, a Bank Holiday or Sunday) the court may specify a period which ends at noon on the first later day which is not a public holiday.

Exclusion Requirements in Emergency Protection Orders [s.44A CA 1989 as inserted by s.52 & Sch.6 FLA 1996]

■ Provisions described below enable the court when making an EPO to attach an exclusion requirement so a suspected abuser can be removed/kept away from the home in which child is living, or the surrounding area.

NB. 'Without notice' orders may offend against Article 6 and especially in attaching exclusion requirements where it may also be argued there is a potential breach of Article 1 Protocol 1 of the Convention (Right to Peaceful Enjoyment of Possessions) i.e. one's home.

■ When the court is satisfied that the threshold criteria for an EPO are satisfied and it makes such an order, the court may also include an exclusion requirement if the following conditions are satisfied:

• There is reasonable cause to believe if the 'relevant person' is excluded from a dwelling-house in which the child lives, the child will not be likely to suffer significant harm either if s/he is not removed (ie. s.44(1)(a)(i)), or does not remain (ie. s.44(1)(a)(ii), or because enquiries as per s.44(1) (b) or (c) will cease to be frustrated

• Another person living in same dwelling-house (parent or not) is able and willing to give to the child the care which it would be reasonable to give her/him and that person consents to the inclusion of the exclusion requirement.

NB. 'An argument could be made in respect of potential breaches of Article 8 and Article 1 Protocol 1 of the Convention, and the proportionality principle previously referred to is also relevant.

- An 'exclusion requirement' for the purposes of s.44A CA 1989 is any one or more of the following provisions:

  - Requiring the relevant person to leave a dwelling-house in which s/he is living with a child
  - Prohibiting the relevant person from entering a dwelling-house in which the child lives
  - Excluding the relevant person from a defined area in which a dwelling-house in which the child lives is situated [s.44A(5) CA 1989 as inserted by s.52 & Sch.6 FLA 1996]

Duration of Exclusion Requirement in Emergency Protection Order [s.44A (4) CA 1989 as inserted by s.52 & Sch. 6 FLA 1996]

- The court may provide that the exclusion requirement is to have effect for a shorter period than the other provisions of the order.

NB. There is no power to extend exclusion requirements beyond interim or EPO stage and if continuing protection is sought, an application must be made by person with whom the child living, for an injunction under s.100 or perhaps a Prohibited Steps Order.

Power of Arrest [s.44A (5) CA 1989 as inserted by s.52 & Sch.6 FLA 1996]]

▪ The exclusion requirement may have a power of arrest attached to it [s.44A (5)].Where it does so, the court may provide that the power of arrest is to have effect for a shorter period than the exclusion requirement [s.44A (6) CA 1989 as inserted by s.52 & Sch.6 FLA 1996].

NB. Any period specified for the purposes of ss. (4) or (6) may be extended by the court on one or more occasions on an application to vary or discharge the EPO [s.44A (7) CA 1989 as inserted by s.52 & Sch.7 FLA 1996].

▪ When a power of arrest is attached to an exclusion requirement of an EPO, a constable may arrest without warrant any person whom s/he has reasonable grounds to believe to be in breach of the requirement [s.44A(8) CA 1989 as inserted by s.52 & Sch.6 FLA 1996].

▪ If while an EPO containing an exclusion requirement is in force, the applicant has removed the child from the dwelling-house from which the relevant person is excluded, to other accommodation for a continuous period of over 24 hours, the order shall cease to have effect in so far as it imposes the exclusion requirement [s.44A (10) CA 1989 as inserted by s.52 & Sch.6 FLA 1996].

Undertakings Relating to Emergency Protection Orders [s.44B CA 1989 as inserted by s.52 & Sch.6 FLA 1996]

- In any case where the court has power to include an exclusion requirement in an EPO, the court may accept an undertaking from the relevant person and in such cases no power of arrest may be attached [s.44B(1) & (2) CA 1989 as inserted by s.52 & Sch.6 FLA 1996].

- Such an undertaking:
  - Is enforceable as if it were an order of the court
  - Will cease to have effect if, whilst it is in force, the applicant has removed the child from the dwelling-house from which relevant person is excluded to other accommodation for a continuous period of more than 24 hours [s.44B(3) CA 1989 as inserted by s.52 & Sch.6 FLA 1996]

- On the application of a person who is not entitled to apply for the order to be discharged, but is a person to whom an exclusion requirement contained in the order applies, an EPO may be varied or discharged by the court in so far as it imposes the exclusion requirement [s.45(8A) CA 1989 as inserted by s.52 & Sch.6 FLA 1996].

- When a power of arrest has been attached to an exclusion requirement of EPO the court may, on the application of any person entitled to apply for the discharge of the order so far as it imposes the exclusion requirement, vary or discharge the order in so far as it confers a power of arrest (regardless of whether any application has been made to vary or discharge any other provision of the order) [s.45 (8B) CA 1989 as inserted by s.52 & Sch.6 FLA 1996].

Challenge of EPO

- An application for a discharge can be made by parent, person with parental responsibility, child or anyone with whom child living at time of EPO.

- So as to ensure compatibility with the European Convention on Human Rights, s.30 C&YPA 2008 revoked the previous 72 restriction on applying for a discharge of an EPO.

  NB. Reasonable contact is assumed between child and above parties and can only be restricted by court direction. A court may be asked for/may give directions to limit contact and/or about medical/ psychiatric examinations. A child of 'sufficient understanding' or aged 16 or over may refuse examination.

Discovery [s.48 (1) Children Act 1989]

- If necessary, a court may direct someone to disclose to applicant for EPO the whereabouts of a child.

- *A statement or admission made in complying with a court direction to disclose a child's whereabouts is not admissible in evidence against person or spouse in proceedings other than perjury.*

Entry/ Search [s.48 (3) Children Act 1989]

- An EPO may include directions to enter and search (but not by force).

Warrant [s.48 (9) & (10) Children Act 1989]

- Where a court believes applicant has been/is likely to be refused access to child it may issue a warrant to police to assist, using if necessary, reasonable force.

  NB. The court can direct that police be accompanied by a doctor, nurse or health visitor.

Police Powers of Protection (PPOP) [s.46 Children Act 1989]

Grounds [s.46(1)]

■ Police must have reasonable grounds to believe child would otherwise suffer 'significant harm'.

NB. PPOP may arguably breach Article 8(1)(Right To Respect for Private and Family Life). Although Article 8(2) qualifies this right, the public authority's interference must be 'proportionate'.

Effect

■ A PPOP.:

- Allows a police constable to remove and accommodate child, or
- Ensures that s/he remains in current location
- Does not give parental responsibility
- Does allow police to do all that is reasonable

Duration [s.46(6)]

■ Up to 72 hours.

Conditions

■ Police must:

- Inform parent, local authority and child of steps taken [s.46 (3) and (4)], and

- Transfer her/him as soon as possible to local authority accommodation, though the responsibility for ongoing enquiries and any decision to release child from police protection remains with the Police

NB. Police can also apply for an EPO to be made in favour of a local authority. Any time spent in police protection must be deducted from time on EPO

Recovery Order [s.50 Children Act 1989]

Applications

- Local authority, NSPCC and Police if child on EPO or CO (including interim CO).

- Police if subject of PPOP

Grounds

- Child is subject to Care Order, EPO or in Police protection, has run away or is being kept away from a responsible person who should be caring for her/him, or is missing

Effect

- Directs responsible person to produce child or to inform of whereabouts.

- Authorises Police to search (using reasonable force if necessary), and

- Allows removal of child by authorised person.

Refuges [s.51 Children Act 1989]

- If foster carers, private or voluntary homes have a certificate from the Secretary of State, they are exempt from law covering abduction of children.

Child Assessment Order (CAO) [s.43 Children Act 1989]

Application

▪ By local authority or NSPCC [s.43 (1) CA 1989]

NB. Applicant must provide 7 days' notice to persons listed in s.43 (11) and a court can treat the application as if it were for an EPO [s.43 (3) CA 1989].

Grounds [s.43 (1)]

▪ Applicant must satisfy the court that s/he has reasonable cause to suspect child is suffering or is likely to suffer 'significant harm', and

- Needs an assessment of the state of the child's health or development or way in which s/he has been treated to determine if s/he is suffering or likely to suffer 'significant harm', and that the
- Assessment is otherwise unlikely to be undertaken or to be satisfactory

NB. For a case where a local authority was reluctant to pay for a court ordered assessment but the House of lords ordered it to proceed se Re C (Interim Care Order: Residential Assessment) [1997] 1 FLR.

Effect [s.43 (6)]

■ Obliges person/s to produce child and comply with court directions e.g. medicals and any other form of assessment – see Re C [1997] 1 FLR 1 [HL].

NB. If of sufficient understanding or aged 16 or over, a child may refuse medical. If necessary, child may be kept from home.

Duration [s.43 (6)]

■ From a specified date and for such period, not exceeding 7 days, which may be specified.

Rights of Refusal of Medical & Other Assessment [ss.38; 43; 44 CA 1989]

■ The right of a child to refuse to submit to medical, psychiatric or dental investigations is limited to the assessment stages of the order provided for the above sections.

NB. For the circumstances in which the child's refusal may be overruled, see South Glamorgan CC v W and B [1993] 1 FLR 574 where the High Court's inherent jurisdiction under s.100 CA 1989 was invoked to override the refusal of a 15 year old to psychiatric assessment in an interim Care Order s.38(6) direction.

APPENDICES

Appendix 1: Convention Rights and Fundamental Freedoms [Articles 2-12 and 14 of Convention, Articles 1-3 First Protocol and Articles 1 and 2 Sixth Protocol, as read with Articles 16–18 of Convention]

With effect from 02.10.00, all courts in England and Wales have been required, so far as is possible to interpret all legislation, whenever enacted, in a way which is compatible with the European Convention on Human Rights.

It is unlawful for public authorities to act in a way which is incompatible with Convention rights summarised in the following pages.

When introducing legislation, government must make a statement about the compatibility of the Bill with Convention rights.

'The HRA 1998 is the most significant statement of human rights in the UK since the 1689 Bills of Rights (a statement by the then Home Office Minister Paul Boateng 26.11.99).

Articles 2–12 & 14

Article 2 – Right to Life

Everyone's right to life shall be protected by law and no one shall be deprived of her/his life intentionally except in the execution of a sentence of a court following her/his conviction of a crime for which this penalty is provided in law.

This Article is not contravened if force, no more than absolutely necessary is used:

a). In defence of any person from unlawful violence

b). In order to effect a lawful arrest or to prevent the escape of a person lawfully detained

c). In action lawfully taken for the purpose of quelling a riot or insurrection

Relevant cases: Osman v UK [1999] 1 FLR 193, Keenan v UK (21 May 2001) EHRR 2001.

Article 3 – Prohibition of Torture

No one shall be subjected to torture or to inhuman or degrading treatment or punishment.

Relevant case: A v UK [1998] 2 FLR 959.

Article 4 – Prohibition of Slavery and Forced Labour

No one shall be held in slavery or servitude.

No one shall be required to perform forced or compulsory labour.

'Forced' or 'compulsory' labour excludes work required in the ordinary course of detention in accordance with Article 5 [see below] or during conditional release from such detention; any military service or its equivalent for conscientious objectors; any service exacted in the case of an emergency or calamity which threatens life or well being of the community; any work or service which forms part of normal civic obligations.

Article 5 – Right to Liberty & Security

1. Everyone has the right to liberty and security of person. No one shall be deprived of liberty except in the following cases and in accordance with a procedure described in law:

a). Lawful detention of a person after conviction by a competent court.

b). Lawful arrest or detention of a person for non-compliance with the lawful order of a court or in order to secure the fulfilment of any obligation prescribed below.

c). Lawful arrest or detention to bring a person before the competent legal authority on reasonable suspicion of having committed an offence (or when it is reasonably considered necessary to prevent her/him committing an offence or from fleeing having done so).

d). Detention of a minor by lawful order for purpose of educational supervision or lawful detention so as to bring her/him before the competent legal authority.

e). Lawful detention of persons for the prevention of the spreading of infectious diseases, of persons of unsound mind, alcoholics, drug addicts or vagrants.

f). Lawful arrest or detention of a person to prevent her/him effecting an unauthorised entry into the country or of a person against whom action is being taken with a view to deportation or extradition.

2. Everyone who is arrested must be informed promptly in a language s/he understands of the reasons and of any charges against them.

3. Everyone arrested/detained in accordance with para.1.c). above, must be brought promptly before a judge or another officer authorised by law to exercise judicial power and is entitled to trial within a reasonable period of time, or release pending trial or release may be conditioned by guarantees to appear for trial.

4. Everyone who is deprived of liberty by arrest/detention is entitled to take proceedings by which the lawfulness of her/his detention is decided speedily by a court and release ordered if the detention is not lawful.

5. Everyone who has been the victim of arrest/detention in contravention of the provisions of this Article has an enforceable right to compensation.

Article 6 – Right to Fair Trial

1. In the determination of her/his civil rights and obligations or of any criminal charge against them, everyone is entitled to a fair and public hearing within a reasonable time by an independent and impartial tribunal established by law. Judgement must be given publicly but the press and public may be excluded from all or part of the trial in the interests of morals, public order or national security in a democratic society; where the interests of juveniles or the protection of the private life of the parties require it; or to the extent strictly necessary in the court's opinion in special circumstances where publicity would prejudice the interests of justice.

2. Everyone charged with a criminal offence must be presumed innocent until proved guilty according to law.

3. Everyone charged with a criminal offence has the following minimum rights:

a). To be informed promptly in a language s/he understands in detail of the nature and reason for the accusation.

b). To have adequate time and facilities for preparation of defence.

c). To defend her/himself in person or through legal assistance of the person's choosing, or if of insufficient means to pay for legal assistance to be given it free when the interests of justice require it.

d). To examine or have examined witnesses against her/him and to obtain the attendance and examination of witnesses on her/his behalf under the same conditions as witnesses against her/him.

e). To have the free assistance of an interpreter if s/he cannot understand or speak the language used in court.

Relevant case: Re A (Separate Representation) [2001] 1 FLR 715 and Re M (Care: Challenging Decision by a Local Authority) [2001] 2 FLR 1300.

Article 7 – No Punishment without Law

1. No one must be held guilty of any criminal offence on account of any act or omission which did not constitute a criminal offence under national or international law at the time when it was committed. Nor must a heavier penalty be imposed than the one which was applicable at the time the criminal offence was committed.

2. This Article must not prejudice the trial and punishment of any person for any act or omission which at the time it was committed was criminal according to the general principles of law recognised by civilised nations.

Article 8 – Right to Respect for Private & Family Life

1. Everyone has the right to respect for her/his private and family life, home and correspondence.

2. There must be no interference by a public authority with the exercise of this right except such as is in accordance with the law and is necessary in a democratic

society in the interests of national security, public safety or the economic well being of the country, for the prevention of disorder or crime, for the protection of health or morals, or for the protection of the rights and freedoms of others.

Relevant cases: Hendrik v Netherlands [1982] 5 EHRR 223 – children's interests will always prevail over parents' rights to private and family life endorsed in Dawson v Wearmouth [1999] 1 FLR 1167 and reported by Court of Appeal in Re L, V, M and H [2000] 2 FLR 334 when Butler-Sloss stated 'in particular, the parent cannot be entitled under Article 8 of the Convention to have such measures taken as would harm child's health and development'.

Article 9 – Freedom of Thought, Conscience & Religion

1. Everyone has the right to freedom of thought, conscience and religion; this freedom includes freedom to change religion or belief and freedom either alone or in community with others and in public or in private, to manifest her/his religion or belief in worship, teaching, practice and observance.

2. Freedom to manifest one's religion or beliefs shall be subject to such limitations as are prescribed by law and are necessary in a democratic society in the interests of public safety, for the protection of public order, health or morals, or for the protection of the rights and freedoms of others.

Relevant case: Re J (Muslim Circumcision Specific Issue Order) [2000] 1 FLR 571.

Article 10 – Freedom of Expression

1. Everyone has the right of freedom of expression. This right shall include freedom to hold opinions and to receive and impart information and ideas without interference by public authority and regardless of frontiers. This Article shall not prevent States from requiring the licensing of broadcasting, television or cinema enterprises.

2.The exercise of these freedoms, since it carries with it duties and responsibilities may be subject to such formalities, conditions, restrictions or penalties as are prescribed by law and are necessary in a democratic society in the interest of national security, territorial integrity or public safety, for the protection of disorder or crime, for the protection of health or morals, for the protection of the reputation or rights of others, for preventing the disclosure of information received in confidence or for maintaining the authority and impartiality of the judiciary.

Article 11 – Freedom of Assembly & Association

1. Everyone has the right to freedom of peaceful assembly and to freedom of association with others including the right to form and join trades unions for the protection of her/his interests.

2. No restrictions shall be placed on the exercise of these rights other than such as are prescribed by law an are necessary in a democratic society in the interests of national security or public safety, for the prevention of disorder or crime or for the protection of the rights and freedoms of others. This Article shall not prevent the imposition of lawful restrictions on the exercise of these rights by members of the armed forces, of the police or of the administration of the State.

Article 12 – Right to Marry

Men and women of marriageable age have the right to marry and to found a family according to the national laws governing the exercise of that right.

Article 14 – Prohibition of Discrimination

The enjoyment of the rights and freedoms set forth in this Convention shall be secured without discrimination on any ground such as sex, race, colour, language, religion, political or other opinion, national or social origin, association with a national minority, property, birth or other status.

Breach of Article 14 cannot be argued on its own but must be linked with some other breach of a Convention Article e.g. Breach of Right To A Fair Trial' such as an argument that denying children rights to representation in residence and contact proceedings is based on discrimination on the grounds of age (Articles 6 and 14.

Articles 1- 3 First Protocol

Article 1 – Protection of Property

Every natural or legal person is entitled to the peaceful enjoyment of their possessions. No one shall be deprived of their possessions except in the public interest and subject to conditions provided for by law and the general principles of international law (this does not impair the right of the State to enforce necessary laws on use of property or to secure payment of taxes or other contributions or penalties).

Article 2 – Right to Education

No person shall be denied the right to education. In the exercise of any functions which it assumes in relation to education and teaching, the State shall respect the rights of parents to ensure such education and teaching in conformity with their own religious and philosophical convictions.

Article 3 – Right to Free Elections

Signatory States undertake to hold free elections at reasonable intervals by secret ballot under conditions which will ensure the free expression of the opinion of the people in the choice of the legislature.

Articles 1 & 2 Sixth Protocol

Article 1- Abolition of Death Penalty

The death penalty shall be abolished. No one shall be condemned to such penalty or executed.

Article 2- Death Penalty in time of War

A State may make provision in its law for the death penalty in respect of acts committed in time of war or of its imminent threat (such a penalty must be applied in accordance with a national law and the State must communicate the relevant provision to the Secretary General of the Council of Europe).

> *NB: All the above rights and freedoms must be read with Articles 16–18 of the Convention which are as follows.*

Articles 16-18 Convention Rights & Freedoms

Article 16 – Restrictions on Political Activity of Aliens

Nothing in Articles 10, 11 &14 shall be regarded as preventing the signatories from imposing restrictions on the political activity of aliens.

Article 17- Prohibition of Abuse of Rights

Nothing in this Convention may be interpreted as implying for any State, group or person any right to engage in any activity or perform any act aimed at the destruction of any of the rights and freedoms set forth

herein, or at their limitation to a greater extent than is
provided for in the Convention.

Article 18 – Limitation on Use of Restriction of Rights

Restrictions permitted under this Convention to the said
rights and freedoms shall not be applied for any purpose
other than those for which they have been prescribed.

Designated Derogation and Reservation

Convention Articles summarised in preceding pages are to have effect for the purposes of HRA 1998, subject to any:

- *'Designated Derogation'* [time limited capacity for the Secretary of State to suspend either Article 5(3) (arrest and detention under right to liberty and security) or any other specified Article or Protocol] [s.14 HRA 1998], or
- *'Designated Reservation'* [i.e. the UK's reservation about the Education provision implied by Protocol 1 Article 2, second sentence which is elaborated upon in Part 11 of Sch.3] [s.15 HRA 1998] or
- *Other reservation* set out in an order made by the Secretary of State

The Secretary of State may be order make such amendments to this Act as s/he considers appropriate to reflect the effect, in relation to the UK of a Protocol to the convention which the UK has ratified or has signed with a view to ratification [s.1(4) &(5)]. No amendment may be made by such an order so as to come into force before the Protocol concerned is in force in the UK [s.1 (6)].

Appendix 2: Human Rights Act 1998

Interpretation of Convention Rights [s.2 HRA 1998]

■ A court or tribunal determining a question which has arisen in connection with a Convention right must take into account in accordance with rules, any relevant judgement, decision, declaration or advisory opinion of the European Court of Human Rights, opinion or decision formally provided by the Commission or any decision made by the Committee of Ministers.

Interpretation of Legislation [s.3 HRA 1998]

■ So far as it is possible to do so, primary and subordinate legislation must be read and given effect in a way which is compatible with Convention rights.

■ The above provision applies:

- Whenever the primary and subordinate legislation was enacted and
- Does not affect validity, continuing operation or enforcement of any incompatible primary legislation and
- Does not affect the validity, continuing operation or enforcement of any incompatible subordinate legislation if (disregarding any possibility of revocation) primary legislation prevents removal of the incompatibility

Declaration of Incompatibility [s.4 HRA 1998]

■ If a court determines that the provision of primary or subordinate legislation is incompatible with a Convention right, it may make a declaration of that incompatibility [s.4 (1)–(3) HRA 1998].

NB. Court in this section means House of Lords, Judicial Committee of the Privy Council, Courts Martial Appeal Court and in England and the High Court or the Court of Appeal [s.4(5) HRA 1998]

■ A declaration of incompatibility:

- Does not affect the validity, continuing operation or enforcement of the provision in respect of which it is given and
- Is not binding on the parties to the proceedings in which it is made [s.4(6) HRA 1998]

NB. Where a court is considering whether to make a declaration of incompatibility, the Crown is entitled to notice in accordance with rules of court and may be joined as a party to the proceedings [s.5 HRA 1998].

Act of Public Authorities [s.6 (1) HRA 1998]

■ It is unlawful for a 'public authority' to act in a way which is incompatible with a Convention right

NB. A public authority includes a court or tribunal and any person certain of whose functions are functions of a public nature, but does not include either House of Parliament or a person exercising

functions in connection with proceedings in Parliament.

- A person who claims that a public authority has acted (or proposes to act) in a way which is made unlawful by s.6(1) may:

    - Bring proceedings against the authority under this Act in the appropriate court or tribunal or
    - Rely on the Convention right/s concerned in any legal proceedings,
    - But only if s/he is (or would be) a victim of the unlawful act [s.7 (1)]

NB. Time limits do or may, in accordance with rules of court be applied to bringing such proceedings [s.1(5)] which may only be brought exercising a right of appeal on an application for judicial review or in such courts may be prescribed in rules [s.9(1)].

Power to Take Remedial Action [s.10 HRA 1998]

- If a provision of legislation has been declared to be incompatible with a Convention right and:

    - All those eligible to appeal confirm in writing that they do not intend to do so, the time limit has expired or an appeal initiated has been determined or
    - The Crown determines that to achieve compatibility with European Convention obligations, primary or secondary legislation needs amending

- A Minister of the Crown may by order make such amendments as s/he considers necessary

Freedom of Thought, Conscience & Religion [s.13 HRA 1998]

■ If a court (including a tribunal) determines that any question arising under this Act might affect the exercise by a religious organisation (itself or its members collectively) of the Convention right to freedom of thought, conscience and religion it must have particular regard to the importance of that right.

Parliamentary Statement of Compatibility [s.19 HRA 1998]

■ A Minister of the Crown in charge of a Bill in either House of Parliament must before second reading of that Bill:

- Make a written statement to the effect that the Bill's provisions are compatible with the Convention's rights or
- Make a written statement to the effect that although s/he is unable to make a statement of compatibility, the government nevertheless wishes to proceed with the Bill

Appendix 3: CAE Publications

Personal Guides From CAE Ltd Pantiles Langham Road Robertsbridge East Sussex TN32 5EP tel: 01580 880243 email: childact@caeuk.org or order via our secure on-line facility at www.caeuk.org

- Children Act 1989 & Child Protection
- Fostering
- Residential Care

www.caeuk.org

Discounts on orders of 50 or more of any one title

Subject Index

P